Reality and Career Planning

A guide for personal growth

Nicholas W. Weiler

Reality and Career Planning

A guide for personal growth

Addison-Wesley Publishing Company

Reading, Massachusetts • Menlo Park, California
Don Mills, Ontario • Wokingham, England • Amsterdam
Sydney • Singapore • Tokyo • Mexico City • Bogotá
Santiago • San Juan

Acknowledgment is made to the International Transactional Analysis Association for permission to reprint material from Stephen Karpman, "Fairy Tales and Script Drama Analysis" from *Transactional Analysis Journal* 7, No. 26 (pp. 39–43); Franklin Ernst, Jr., "The OK Corral: The Grid for Get on With" from *Transactional Analysis Journal* 1, No. 4 (pp. 33–42); Taibi Kahler with Hedges Capers, "The Miniscript" from *Transactional Analysis Journal* 4, No. 1 (pp. 26–42); and Stephen Karpman, "Options" from *Transactional Analysis Journal* 1, No. 1 (pp. 79–87).

Seventh Printing, October 1984

To My Wife, Claire

and to my children: Tim,
Ann,
Chris,
Kevin,
Maura

whose understanding and support during
the long months of writing made it possible to
turn this book from dream to reality.

Thank you. You were super!

If we should each march to our own drum . . .

How do I find the drummer?

If I have an uneasy feeling that I'm out of step . . .

Where do I listen for the beat?

Preface

The majority of adults in this country *hate their work*. Whether it is a factory job, a white collar job, or with some exceptions a professional job, or the role of being a housewife, they hate their work as much as young people rebel at the prospect of similar work; indeed it is the parents' feelings that are a principal source of the children's feelings. The middle class also resents the authority that is imposed by work—the boss and the system—and *they feel that they lack power over their own lives.**

Not everyone will agree in total with the above statement, but most of us can identify with parts of it. Many people like segments of their jobs—perhaps the technical, artistic, or creative dimensions—but not their whole jobs.

Most of us hate feelings of being trapped and limited by our work, particularly after we've mastered it and it's becoming repetitive. No one can deny that many in our population have always hated most parts of their jobs, and endured work from the beginning as a necessary evil to earn a living. When they go to work, the self stays at home. It's a split and frustrating existence. Frustration is fatiguing, sometimes so much so that there is no energy left for the self even at home. Starved, the self slips away and is forgotten.

Of all the forms of impoverishment that can be seen or felt in America, loss of self, or death in life, is surely the most devastating.†

---

* From Charles A. Reich, *The Greening of America* (New York: Bantam Books, 1971), p. 296. Reprinted by permission of Random House, Inc.
† Ibid., p. 7.

No one wants to "feel that they lack power over their own lives." Yet this feeling is epidemic in our organizational systems. The bosses feel it as much as the subordinates, and it is to no one's advantage. It is demotivating and de-energizing at a time when the productivity that depends on people's energy and motivation is critical to the economic survival of both the individual and the organization.

Is this situation hopeless? Are lack of personal power and dislike of work the inevitable consequences of employment in large organizations or can we, as individuals, do something to improve things for ourselves? Must we wait passively for organizations to improve?

The answer, fortunately, is that we needn't wait. After making a careful effort to look, I've found that powerlessness is not inevitable. There are many people who are having fun and enthusiastically pursuing their own personal values within organizations today. Their ranks are growing and they are not trying to change the establishment or fight existing systems. They've discovered that this is unnecessary. They've learned that autonomy and potency are possible within most organizations the way they are.

The key lies in developing a clear awareness of how most organizational systems *really do* operate, as opposed to being blinded by naive expectations about how they are *supposed to* operate, and then designing a personal program for dealing with the realities observed. Awareness has become a powerful tool for many in a world of unaware and frustrated contemporaries.

These people are not revolutionaries and they are not necessarily young. Many are older, highly successful professionals and managers. Most are friendly people with high integrity and hard-won self-assurance. They are fun to be around and they accomplish a lot.

I like these people—and I've been watching what they do.

I began watching several years ago when I was emerging from a long period of working with stunned professionals who had unexpectedly found themselves out of work in the engineering cutbacks of the late sixties. I had seen hundreds of grown men, some with twenty and more years of strong performance behind them, suddenly become like helpless children. They did not understand what had happened to them. It seemed unreal. They had done everything they'd been asked to do and, for the first time, the organization was not going to reward them. Instead they were being laid off—they were being told they were on their own to fend for themselves with no practice and no skills at doing that.

For many, as they looked back, their entire work life since college began to seem unreal. They realized they had never had much control over what happened to them; they'd been running too fast to notice where they were going. They'd been so busy responding to what they thought the organization valued that they'd never taken time to define any clear values of their own. Now the organization was rejecting them. Did that mean they should reject themselves? That subtle but essential question became even more critical than the loss of income. Could self-esteem survive the loss of organizational esteem?

Most eventually but painfully found jobs and grew from the experience. Many established a new, more secure self-esteem based on self-sufficiency rather than on organizational recognition and reward. They developed better defined priorities in life and an improved contact with themselves, their personal values, and their families. It was surprising to some that their worth at home was not a function of their professional status. Their families were interested in what kinds of human beings they were, not in what they did for a living. Their children appreciated them more, not less, for admitting their anxieties.

In retrospect, the crisis was a good thing for many. I began to feel they were in subtle ways better off than the millions of Americans who have never faced an economic crisis. Most people are still running mindlessly with no time or necessity to stop and notice—to become aware of themselves and their needs as persons, to define their personal values, and to learn how values can be realized or destroyed within organizational systems.

I began to notice a great deal more myself—to look beyond the surface cliches and search out the facts about how the system works for and against people in organizations. I wrote this book to share what I discovered.

This is not a book about domineering corporations, government bureaucracies, or the evils of the establishment in general. This is a book about you, an individual who has to survive and who wants to achieve something of value in life and on the job in spite of all the problems imperfect organizations and systems may bring your way.

I'm optimistic. I believe systems and organizations are gradually improving. My grandchildren will be better off than I am.

I'm selfish too. I don't want to leave all the fun for my grandchildren. I want some fun and self-fulfillment for myself too—now. I want to enjoy my work and feel that it is meaningful. I want to grow as a person on the job in dimensions that are important to me. I want to come home from work relaxed rather than frustrated so I can notice and enjoy all the other good things in life.

How about you? What do you want, and how are you going to make certain you get it? This book won't answer those questions for you, but I will show you how to answer them for yourself.

Fairfield, Connecticut   N.W.W.
November 1976

Acknowledgments

This book was in process over two years, and I can never give sufficient thanks to all the people who contributed to my motivation and the clarification of my thinking as the manuscript evolved through several successive drafts.

To mention only a few, I give particular thanks to Fritz Metzger, Lew Sears, and Dave Barber who told me I had something to say and encouraged me to write it down; to Helene Aronson and Mary and Bob Goulding who taught me Transactional Analysis and gave me the insights needed to apply it in organizations; to Herb Hamsher whose critiques, enthusiasm, and candid challenges to really finish the job contributed immeasurably; to Paul Moyer who told me to get organized; and to Tony Petrella, Neale Clapp, and Mike Hill who taught me so much about the interpersonal communications dimension of *Process* and its importance in organizations.

I also want to thank Addison-Wesley's anonymous manuscript readers. Your straightforward criticisms, and your obvious caring in taking the time to give them, helped make the final draft a much better product.

Contents

Exercises

Introduction

How do I find the drummer?

"What do you want to do?" The man was 45 years old and he couldn't answer the question. He couldn't really answer it, that is . . . at least not to himself.

He could give the expected answer, mouth the expected jargon. He knew the game and the executive recruiter across the table knew he knew it. He'd been playing the game, well, since his first campus interview with the corporate recruiter during his senior year. That was over 20 years ago. By now he was an expert at anticipating questions and giving the expected answers. Why wasn't it working anymore?

He was intelligent, very intelligent. He'd never had to worry about that. And he was well educated, with a bachelor's in Engineering and a master's in Business Administration. He had all the right credentials, but somehow that knowledge didn't satisfy him as much as it once did.

This was the first time since his campus interview that he'd sought out a recruiter. Why did he bother? He'd never had to look for a job, and he didn't have to look now. Why was he even here? He'd been with the company since college. Why look outside now? It was probably too late anyway.

That's what really seemed to be bothering him. It was getting late. But late for what?

He'd never had to look for a job because he'd been successful. He'd changed jobs and he'd moved ahead, but he'd never had to look. The jobs had always come to him. He believed the company recognized and rewarded good performers. That was the system. He'd worked hard and done what was expected of him in every assignment. He'd never had to look.

He hoped this guy understood that now. He didn't have to look for a job.

Why was he reluctant to play the game here? Why was it becoming so fatiguing to create the right impression, to sell himself? He used to enjoy this type of verbal sparring, even looked forward to it. Maybe he was getting old. Maybe the recruiter was just too young. He'd expected an older man in an executive recruiting role. What could this kid know? Well, if this was part of the test, he'd show he was up to it.

"I want an increased challenge. I know my current job too well. I'm busy, but it's lost its excitement. I need some new problems to get my juices going again."

The recruiter wasn't surprised. Young as he was, this was a familiar story to him. He called it the smorgasbord phenomenon. "Don't ask me what I want. Show me the smorgasbord and let me pick." The recruiter stuck to his guns.

"What kind of challenge?"

"What's available?"

"That depends on what you're looking for."

"If you tell me what's available, I'll know whether or not I want it."

It was a long conversation, but not a productive one. At the end he left his resume. He didn't hear from them.

He didn't get an answer to the question that had really brought him there either, because he didn't ask it. He came wondering why his company had just asked him to work for a man who was eight years younger.

He couldn't understand why that should happen. He felt an uneasy sense of loss—uneasy but strangely familiar, as though the loss had been there, hidden, a long time. Somehow the loss involved more than this one missed promotion.

He wanted to know what he'd done wrong. At some level, though he couldn't verbalize it even to himself, he wanted to learn. He wanted to take a new look, maybe even a first look, at what he really wanted in life and discover whether there was anything he could do to make it happen.

The answer was yes, but he wasn't going to find it this way. He was looking for his own identity in the wrong place—he was looking outside himself. He should have been looking within himself, but that's easy to say and hard to do. Most of us have never learned how.

If we should each march to our own drum ...
HOW DO I FIND THE DRUMMER?

If I have an uneasy feeling that I'm out of step ...
WHERE DO I LISTEN FOR THE BEAT?

Autonomy is learnable

Does the above scene sound familiar? Have you ever been in a similar situation, either as the interviewee or as a manager conducting an interview? I have. In my role as a manpower consultant I've been engaged in variations of this scene hundreds of times. As a member of the so-called helping professions, I've often been frustrated at my inability to help. I've also been impressed at how some people are able to take charge and help themselves.

Watching these autonomous people, I've discovered that what they do isn't mysterious, although it is relatively rare. Few people in our culture understand the techniques of autonomy, the basic fundamentals of how to identify and maintain self in an increasingly depersonalized environment. When you finish this book I believe you'll understand these techniques, and I hope you'll decide to use them for yourself.

As author, I'll provide you with information, tools, methodology, and specific exercises you can use to take charge of your career and get what you want. That is what you can expect of me.

I ask you, the reader, for your energy in reading and your active participation in thinking about and answering the questions I suggest you ask yourself. I ask for your honesty in your answers (no one will see them but you) and your open-mindedness about where each chapter is leading you. These are my expectations.

The process we'll be working through as you progress does have a design, a flow that ties the separate parts into a unified whole. Individual sections are meant to raise questions before they discuss answers. This is deliberate. It is a participative learning process.

In the end, the search for relevance to your own career and life will naturally be your own. I rely a great deal on your individual intelligence and ability to pick and choose what will be useful to you.

The various exercises in this book rely on your willingness to look at your own motivations and answer tough questions about your values. Obviously some will choose not to do this. That's OK too. There's no law that says everyone has to face the tough job of honestly looking at what values he or she wants to realize in life. Most people don't.

I believe your work life can be much more rewarding if you do face this task. I feel the rewards are worth the efforts. That's my value, however. If nothing else, I hope this book helps you realize the importance of setting your own values. We'll be devoting a whole chapter to value tradeoffs.

Eight parts

The book is divided into eight parts, each dealing with a different basic building block for effective career planning to achieve career goals.

PART 1 discusses the *realities* of career planning as it exists— or doesn't exist—in most organizations today. This section covers career realities (and myths), organization realities, communication (and noncommunication) realities, the realities of negotiating career contracts that meet the needs of both the individual and the organization, and career-counseling realities.

Clearly, PART 1 presents my perceptions of reality. You'll agree with some of the things I say and disagree with others. In either event, I hope PART 1 makes the point that each of us must fine tune our own antennae and develop a clear, nonmythical awareness of how things really do happen in organizations we deal with. Without this as a solid foundation, any attempts at career planning will be built on sand. My impression is that most career-planning programs, personal and organizational, flounder on well-intentioned myths before they ever get started.

PART 2 covers *finding the drummer*. Here our basic psychological needs are analyzed with emphasis on how these needs can influence whether or not we ever identify what we want to do in life (as opposed to what others want for us). In this section we look at the various roles we play, personality structure, and where to look for the drummer. PART 2 also contains a series of exercises you can use to identify and sort out the various extraneous voices and influences that may be blocking your awareness of what you really want. Finally, you'll see how you can put your own drummer to work at developing a practical set of priorities for what's uniquely important to you in life and on the job.

PART 3 contains a specific step-by-step roadmap for *selecting a career path*. Here you'll find a series of exercises for developing concrete, achievable career goals that will allow you to realize your most important values and do the kinds of things you want to do. This section also analyzes the difference between the tiring busyness of day-to-day repetitive firefighting in life, and the energy-generating excitement that comes when we stop firefighting, take charge, and build a plan for moving in directions we want to go.

PART 4 discusses how to go about *becoming a winner*. Here we look at the challenge of free choice, how to avoid nonproductive career games, how to find time for career planning, creative mistakes, and the difference between winners and losers.

PART 5 presents *market strategies* for finding a job that will allow you to grow along the career path you've selected. Here we look at research findings on how managers hire and what criteria they use. We look at the pros and cons of personal visibility, techniques for developing marketable resumes, and how to become a fail-safe candidate.

PART 6 presents a series of techniques for conducting *successful negotiations* to get what you want on the job. These include maintaining a win-win (as opposed to win-lose) dialogue with management (or the client if you're self-employed); recognizing predictable Negative Drivers and Positive Allowers that influence whether you "get on with" or "get nowhere with" the realization of your career plans; developing interpersonal competence; diagnosing impasses; and generating creative communications options to expand your repertoires for persuasion.

PART 7 looks at *perspectives* and the question of whether or not career planning for personal self-fulfillment is practical in the real world. PART 7 defines personal fulfillment as "identifying my strengths and using my available energies in the most efficient way possible to build visible competence in work dimensions that I find satisfying." Personal fulfillment, then, is not a liberal standard to be used in an artificial battle against a conservative standard of self-reliance. Personal fulfillment and self-reliance, when understood correctly, are synonymous. The theories and techniques in this book should appeal to both liberals and conservatives.

PART 8 summarizes the questions that the various theories and techniques in the book are intended to help you answer on the not easy but nevertheless exciting and rewarding road to *becoming your own Santa Claus.*

Throughout the various chapters you'll find specific suggestions and techniques for use in deciding what you want on the job and getting it. On page xx you'll find an index of exercises you can use alone or in groups to practice the techniques suggested.

This is a "how to" book designed to show you how to assume personal ownership of your own life and career; how to respond effectively to life's challenges with freedom, autonomy, and a *clear awareness of reality;* how to realize the most possible of the values that are uniquely important to you; and how to make certain they are really your values (not someone else's).

I suggest you read through the book once, and then go back and work through those exercises that are most pertinent to you.

Realities

Part **1**

Without a clear awareness of *realities* as a solid foundation, any attempts at career planning will be built on sand.

I believe most career-planning programs—personal and organizational—flounder on myths before they ever get started.

Career realities 1

Awareness is essential (and rare)

My personal values and desires are seldom realized without active and conscious effort on my part. I must do something to make things happen the way I want them to happen. If I work in an organization, the first thing I must do is notice the realities of organizations. Only with this awareness can I avoid dealing with myths and begin developing a practical plan of action to get what I want within an organization. Most of us build career plans on the myths of what we think "should be" rather than on the reality of what "is." One of the first things an aware person looking at today's organizations notices is that a great many people are not very excited about their jobs.

Boredom is epidemic

Do we now have a significant portion of our professional and managerial work force who are:

- Busy but not very challenged (feeling tired but not relaxed or rewarded by their work)?
- Competent but getting bored (feeling irritable and trapped)?
- Responsive to specific demands made on them; but not excited, involved, innovative, growing, or very self-starting (personal-growth and motivational curves flattening out and falling)?
- Survival-oriented (holding on to what they have and taking few risks in the areas of change, creativity, or even saying what they think)?

I believe that we do.

How did this happen? Why are people bored? And why do they put up with it? If intelligent, mature college graduates are expending a significant percentage of their available energies forcing themselves to go to work (and stay there), why don't they leave? Why don't they get new jobs where they can devote more of their productive energies to doing work they like? Some do leave, of course, but more tend to stay. They stand at an immobilizing impasse and deteriorate. Why?

One reason is habit, the habit most of us have of looking to an impersonal system for answers and waiting passively for solutions rather than risk taking action on our own.

How many systems respond? Who ever really asks what you personally want on the job, even if you're a high-level manager? If someone does ask, do they really listen to your answer?

"What do I want to do?" is a question many of us outgrew, or, more accurately, gave up on, long ago. We don't ask it of anyone but kids, and we get uncomfortable if someone asks it of us. We find it difficult to answer, and we don't really expect others to answer it. It's a question teenagers ask and (fortunately or unfortunately) they tend to ask parents how they found the answer. This is one of the reasons many of us find our children's teenage years even more agonizing for us than our own were.

If I'm bored on the job, I often even forget to ask myself what I want. I'm more likely to look for a scapegoat. "They," whoever "they" are, did this to me. The "organization" passed me over. The "system" didn't do its job. All of the above may be correct, even though it doesn't tell the whole story.

No matter how they try, big organizations made up of hundreds or thousands of individuals tend not to be very organized, particularly in such elusive dimensions as defining and achieving life values and career goals for individuals. Manpower systems, even the most well intentioned, are better at meeting organizational needs than individual needs.

An organization is an "it"

Big organizations are not "theys." Big organizations are "its" made up of thousands of "theys" all struggling with limited success to communicate with one another. A successful Ph.D. in his mid-forties once complained to me that he was disappointed his company hadn't developed him more. My flip response was "How can you get mad at it?" He got my point.

It wasn't only a flip answer; it was not a completely fair one. If the "it" is a big organization, "it" more often than not dumbly perpetuates some harmful career-development myths laid down years ago by paternalistic senior executives who naively promised a great deal more than any "it" could realistically deliver—no matter how hard "its" individual managers tried.

Myths are dangerous and misleading

Let's look at some typical well-meaning but dangerously misleading career-development myths "they" in the person of several generations of line and personnel managers have been trying unsuccessfully to deliver on for years. The first is:

Perform well on your current job and the company will take care of your future. In other words, be good, work hard, don't complain, please Daddy and he'll take care of the future.

How can I do that if Daddy is an "it"?

"Its" don't think at that level of detail. Most companies have difficulty planning their long-range survival as organizations, much less the individual future of each employee.

"Its" don't read minds. No company can get inside my head and decide what I personally want in terms of a career and no career can be planned until I've done at least that. Someone has to ask what I "want" and somehow "I," not "it," have to find an answer.

It wouldn't be right for an organization to try to tell me what my personal goals should be anyway. If any company tries to do that I hope I'm smart enough not to listen.

Large companies have several hundred or even several thousand managerial and supervisory employees. Top management can establish policies but top management can't really control the behavior of hundreds of individual personalities in supervisory positions. Some will be smart and some will be dumb. Some will be very interested in their employees' development. Others will be self-centered people, inclined to keep better employees in their groups long after they've outgrown the job. They don't want the effort of training a replacement. Even the smart and interested managers usually don't have very sophisticated career-counseling skills. They often do more harm than good with their efforts. The most beneficial thing most managers naturally feel they can do is develop a subordinate in their own self-image. That may not be what the subordinate has in mind.

No "it" can control that many "theys." No personnel department will ever have the system or the clout to make that many managers work effectively together on the development of individual employees.

As an antidote to the above myth, don't put an "it" in the driver's seat unless you really don't care where you're going. Steer your own course with your brain and senses always alert. Keep your antennae on, navigate by what they tell you, and read the rest of this book as your driver's manual.

Another outmoded but oft-quoted myth is:

Development of subordinates is one of a manager's prime responsibilities.   This is partially true but it must be kept in perspective. If I'm an employee depending on my boss for career help, I must realize the boss's help can only be very limited. Here's why. My boss knows how to get one step ahead of me in his or her own specialized organizational function—period. If that's my final ambition, I may be safe to depend on my boss.

My boss is still trying to find the formula for how to get *two* steps ahead of me in his or her function. He or she may or may not make it.

My boss usually knows little or nothing about how to get ahead in functions other than his or her own. A boss who is an engineering manager probably knows little more than I do about how people become finance, marketing, or personnel managers. A boss who doesn't have a Ph.D. doesn't really know what it takes to get one. A boss who isn't doing research probably won't ever do it.

Unless my boss is a broad multi-functional business manager at the general-manager level, odds are he or she doesn't know how to become one and probably doesn't even know in any detail what people like that really do. He or she may learn, but how long can I wait?

As an antidote to depending unrealistically on the boss's help, I must somehow broaden my data base and implement a plan for broadening myself. This requires direct contact with people who currently hold the type of jobs I aspire to five or ten years from now. Only people who have done the job can accurately tell me what it consists of and what performance it takes to get there.

Personnel people can preach to line managers about developing their employees till doomsday and nothing will happen if they are asking the impossible. Somehow the personnel specialist must create a system and the manager create a climate where individuals can take the reins and coordinate the development of their own careers. Very few personnel people or managers know how to do this yet. Most are still struggling valiantly with well-meaning but misleading myths on the subject.

They all mean well, but don't wait for them. It's unlikely they'll get there in your lifetime.

If you're waiting, you're at an impasse.

Passivity is fatal

"Don't make me specify what I want. Show me the smorgasbord."

The gentleman who avoided saying what he wanted in our introductory chapter was fairly typical of people who have spent ten or more years in any large organization. When outside events such as a reorganization or a reduction in the work force require them to talk with Personnel about finding a new job, they tend to be very non-specific about what they want. They abdicate and answer the question with another question: "What's available?" Somehow, their personal desires don't seem to count, even to them.

There are several reasons for this. First, because they need a job they want to test the waters and collect data before they get specific. They don't want to eliminate themselves from consideration for any opening by giving some hint it might not be what they like.

Unfortunately, this tactic frequently works and people who use it move all smiles into something they end up hating. This is OK as a short-term expedient to keep bread on the table, if they immediately start a new search (inside or outside the organization) for something they want. Too many people retreat into inertia and stay on doing what they don't like in the interests of financial security. Actually it's a temporary and false security.

People who spend a lot of time doing what they don't like frequently end up not being very good at it. They quit growing. Their value to the organization decreases. They become prime candidates for the next layoff.

Another reason people avoid the question is they've become so accustomed to discounting their personal desires they really don't know what they want. It's an unpleasant and difficult dimension to contemplate. Society in general doesn't ask what an individual wants.

The establishment has no expectations

Society teaches us to ask, "What does the Establishment (i.e., the system, organization, institution, or nation) expect?" and mold ourselves to conform.

But the Establishment is not a living, thinking being. The Establishment is just another "it." "Its" rush forward blindly, changing course unpredictably and at dizzying speed.

One year the demand is all for engineers and technologists. A few years later engineers can't find jobs. The fad switches to ecology. Everyone enrolls in oceanography. By the time they get their degrees, oceanography is passé and everyone's into energy. Some years M.B.A.'s or Ph.D's are all the rage. Other years no one wants them. This year's fad is always going to be the definitive one, the one to last. It never does.

The Establishment is fickle and blind. What it expects in the way of skills depends on who is doing what to whom in Washington; the economy; what Russia, France, England, and Germany do to each other; who revolts in South America; the unknown outcome of future national elections; and so on.

Who can predict all that? Who can build a life or a career on it? Who could have predicted during the early flush of the Apollo program that ten years later aerospace would be a bad word?

People who take engineering *only* because that's where the money for new college graduates is often end up being mediocre engineers. If engineering isn't intrinsically interesting for them, they tend to get behind in the state of the art. They waste energy forcing themselves to go to work.

Natural engineers, those whose energy flows freely to the technical with no forcing, pass them by.

Natural engineers and technologists who force themselves to go into management against their will (usually for reasons of status or money) usually don't make good managers. They don't like it. Natural managers pass them up. The frustrated engineer gets behind in technology and doesn't get ahead in management. He or she ends up being neither—or gets smart and switches back, even if it means a cut in pay.

The marketplace promotes people in things they aren't good at only when the fads are in their favor. When the fad passes the demand drops. The work force in a given skill (like engineering) tends to fall back to the level of people who are really good at it. If I'm a recognized top individual in my field and its natural to me, I can usually find a job whether the fad is running up or down. If I'm not a top individual, I may find more exciting jobs in something else I like better. I can cite case after case of delighted people who now find that being laid off in the engineering cutbacks of the late sixties was the best thing that ever happened to them. When it happened, of course, they were despondent.

In the end, the only security is in being one of the best at what we do. We can seldom be the best if we don't like it, even if it's popular.

There is only one predictable reality

In the end, with a nonpredictable Establishment, the only concrete predictable reality is inside the self. What do I like to do? Where does my energy rush naturally with no forcing? That's what I'll do best. That's where I'll have a real competitive edge. That's where I'll have fun, and that's probably my best chance at making a lot of money independent of where the fads go.

The marketplace tends to reward people who are really good at what they do. Even if this doesn't result in a lot of money, so what? If I earn a decent living and spend my 40-60-hour work week having fun, I'm ahead. How many rich people look back and wish they'd made less money and had more fun? Money can't buy back these many hours of my life I spend every week on the job.

If I don't like my job, I probably can't afford to just quit. Few people can. First I have to develop feasible options I do like. That takes hard work, hard thought, time, information, and effective techniques. It also takes persistence; and a willingness to fail now and then, learn from my mistakes, and try again. The following homily illustrates how many smart people never notice or learn from their own mistakes and seldom risk anything, but instead invest their energies unproductively in downgrading others' success.

Some dumb people are smarter than we think (a homily)

Dumb people frequently get what they want through focus and energy. They appear to notice only one door and they attack it in every possible way until they get through. Then they take on the next door. This can eventually, though perhaps painfully, lead to significant personal satisfactions and accomplishments. (See Fig. 1.1.)

Fig. 1.1   Which door?

Bright people are often hindered by seeing too many doors. They never focus. They feel they can do anything they put their attention to, but too many things get their attention. Because things come easily to them, they depend on their ability to fly by the seat of their pants. They don't do their homework; they dissipate their energies winging it through life and leaving too much to chance—or to dumb people.

Bright people often immobilize themselves, saying "Which door . . . which door . . . which door?" They invest great quantities of energy in superficial confusions rather than systematic growth. This can go on for years or lifetimes. It is often accompanied by complaints of feeling underutilized and trapped.

Bright people who get immobilized by the "which door" phenomenon often end up working for dumb people in jobs they don't like.

This can be very frustrating.

Dumb people are often accused by bright people of not caring what's behind the doors. Bright people are very articulate critics.

Bright people usually claim to care what's behind each door they see, but they frequently don't get around to investigating and finding out. It's as though they prefer to wait for automatic doors that open by themselves.

Sometimes bright people are proud. They won't admit it when they don't know something so they don't ask people who do know. Frequently bright people don't do much at all themselves. They'd rather criticize other dumb doers. If they do things themselves, they might become a target for someone else's criticism. Proud bright people don't like that.

Energetic dumb people can't afford this particular brand of pride or passivity. They don't have time for it. They'll ask questions of anyone who'll answer. If they're really energetic they also tend to spend a lot of time doing homework. They're not smart enough to wing it.

Energetic dumb people tend to do more—and consequently experience more failures than many bright people. Dumb people don't have the sophisticated techniques bright people have for blotting out criticism. They notice their mistakes painfully and learn from them. Then they try again, hitting the door with new perspective and increased energy. Dumb people don't tire as easily as bright people.

This is another reason bright people can end up working for dumb people. Sometimes dumb people work harder, know more, and do more.

It's even more frustrating for bright people when they end up working for dumb people who know more than they do.

Bright people should spend a lot of time systematically asking questions, collecting data, looking behind doors, doing things, sometimes failing, learning, and doing again.

This is the only way bright people can eliminate doors they don't want and focus energy effectively on doors they do want.

Dumb people are forced to choose. Bright people can be very condescending about this fact.

Bright people have to force themselves to choose.

Most people I know consider themselves to be bright.

Some people object to the use of the word "dumb" in this homily. They see it as unkind.

Most of us define "dumb" as other people, particularly if they are getting what they want and we aren't. We rationalize our lack of satisfaction as being caused by our intelligence, our broader view of things, even our integrity. Dumb people get what they want because they aren't perceptive enough to notice all the roadblocks that make their success impossible, or they have tunnel vision, or they don't mind making fools of themselves now and then. When all else fails, we decide they are crooked.

Usually successful dumb people are smarter than we think, and many are very honest—particularly with themselves. They are intelligent and objective enough to notice what they don't know; and self-confident enough to admit what they don't know and seek answers. Sometimes bright people never find themselves or do anything.

If bright people confine themselves to safe observation and criticism, and dumb people insist on taking charge, taking risks, and doing things, bright people get more and more to criticize.

Some bright people find this quite satisfying. It enables them to feel more and more indignant, put upon, and persecuted for being bright.

There is a certain nobility in martyrdom—*if* you're smart enough not to notice that your persecutor is *you*.

What a way to lose a self!

It's known as copping out—with finesse and style!

But passive copping out is never quite so satisfying as actively doing something to get what you really want in life.

Waiting for Big Daddy gets you nowhere

Eric Berne, the California psychiatrist who developed the theory and techniques of Transactional Analysis told us most people are waiting passively for Santa Claus or death.[1] Either offers an end to the anxieties of living.

This describes what many of us are doing in our work. We don't like our jobs, and we're waiting for some unknown organizational Big Daddy to change things even though we know deep down that Big Daddy is a dream. Big Daddy is the grown-up corporate or bureaucratic update of our childhood Santa Claus fantasy.

What we don't realize, and what Berne wanted to tell people, is that we can have it within our own power to develop other options.

Who owns my career? Is it the organization, my manager, personnel corporate training, or me? The best way to answer this question is to ask another question.

Who has the most to lose? Obviously I do.

Who is responsible for developing my options? Hasn't that always been the organization's job? Not really.

How can I depend on an "it"? That's Big Daddy again. The only real live person who can define what I want and develop options to get it is I.

Is there an age beyond which it's too late? Yes, the age when I decide to quit trying. Some people have frozen the design at 20. They are too old. Some keep the design open and start new lives at 60 or 80. Churchill and Grandma Moses did this. They were still young.

Corporations and institutions have numerous humane ways of keeping their longer-service employees reasonably whole financially (early retirement options, etc.) after they've quit growing on the job.

Corporations and institutions are not very good at teaching people how to find self-fulfillment, growth, and excitement on or off the job. Somehow we each have to plan that for ourselves.

In making our plans, it's helpful to notice the reality that, while organizations are not very good at helping people find self-fulfillment, neither are they very good at blocking it, even on the job.

Organization
realities 2

Organizations are easily confounded

Reich tells us that:

> The individual who is free of the conventional goals can make an
> amazing amount of independence for himself within any organiza-
> tion, simply because organizations are so cumbersome, inefficient,
> and unable to meet the demands upon them. They are confounded
> by anyone who takes initiatives. In any organization the advan-
> tage is all with whoever acts, because the means for stopping
> action are ill-developed. The organization "has no ideas" and while
> changing the organization itself is very difficult doing something
> new within the organization is certainly possible. . . .[2]

Reich talks about the conventional goals as being the expected
rewards of promotion and official approval.[3] There is a paradox in this.
If being free of these goals makes me more able to do something new
within the organization; it's also true that doing something new makes
me more likely to achieve these goals.

Conformers often survive but seldom prevail

I can survive in many organizations by abdicating my personality and
conforming, but nonpersonalities are not very visible even in organizations when we look at those who manage to get the big rewards.

My observation after more than 15 years of manpower consulting is that the really significant promotions and rewards seldom go to
those who become overly concerned with meeting some organizational
Big Daddy's approval and not rocking the boat. When these people

do achieve high salaries, it's usually in routine, repetitive, not very challenging functions. They don't have much clout or real impact on what directions the organization takes. If, by error, they do get into jobs that require significant decision making, they tend not to last. They quickly get sidetracked, frequently into high-paying, high-sounding nonjobs, because an embarrassed management doesn't know what to do with them.

Paradoxically, the people who are less dominated by concern for approval and rewards tend to end up getting the most of both commodities. People who are more concerned with meaningful results, who realize Big Daddy is an "it," who deal effectively (if not always gently) in the interpersonal dimensions—those who challenge, innovate, risk, and concern themselves with accomplishment rather than approval—tend to generate the type of individual visibility for themselves that brings the most significant rewards.

This is not a phenomenon reserved for youth or the new consciousness. This is how a lot of shrewd old tigers got there years ago. They realized the system was a mindless "it" that they could control to their personal advantage (though not without a few setbacks). They did not see the system as a coherent Big Daddy who had expectations they had to meet.

I may not share the values of the aggressive executive who gets money and power by sheer will power and the sacrifice of other values, but I can't deny the fact that if that's what this individual values, he or she is achieving it. If I have other values, hopefully I won't feel guilty about not achieving the same power and income, or resentful of the fact that someone else has it. I can also observe what successful people do to get what they want in the system and use similar intelligence and techniques to get what I want.

If someone employs unethical techniques, I won't condone those —but my observation is that there are just as many people who got there ethically. The awareness these people have of how to deal with interpersonal communications and accomplish what's important to them is something we can learn from, even if we want to run an arts and crafts shop.

Politics can be positive

People who get what they want are frequently accused of using "politics" as though that were automatically something bad. It needn't be.

If we define politics negatively as unethical compromise, copping out, manipulating destructively, and making closet deals that would stink in the sunlight; then it is definitely bad practice. This is the common definition when the word is used derisively.

If we define politics as an astute awareness of the human dimensions; as reality orientation and sensitivity to the frequently unspoken needs and feelings of others; as noticing and respecting others' ethical but differing values, anxieties, and interpersonal styles; as concern for the best possible solutions incorporating the best of everyone's ideas (as opposed to a defensive not-invented-here syndrome); and as a carefully, consciously developed set of interpersonal competencies for taking all of the above into account when we want to accomplish change or improvement—politics can be very positive.

We tend to confuse the positive with the negative politicians, particularly when the very human feeling of envy gets involved in judgments made by people who have not learned the legitimate importance of understanding others' feelings and dealing with the interpersonal dimensions of communicating in organizations.

We should be careful to keep the negative and positive politicians separate in our thinking. We can learn a lot from the positive politicians.

Not accepting or understanding the critical realities of interpersonal communications on the job is perhaps the most common roadblock to realizing career goals.

Communica-
tions realities   3

How positive politicians communicate

Somehow the positive politicians have developed very effective inter-personal communications skills. This does not mean that they are flat-terers or con artists. More often it means they have learned how to say no without cutting off further dialogue. They've learned how to get others, and groups, to seek the facts behind conflict and differing opinions with an eye toward productive resolution rather than divi-sive, defensive infighting and one-upmanship. They've learned how to introduce necessary change when most of the organization prefers the more comfortable flow of the status quo. They've also learned how to persist with flexibility in the face of often overwhelming resistance to new ideas or programs that require the cooperation of other people—even their bosses—who didn't invent the ideas and want no part of them.

Being right can be irrelevant

Several years ago I saw a classic example of how important communi-cations ability is for anyone who wants to accomplish something in organizations. I was reading a report on an unusually bright individ-ual I had sent to a large corporation's talent-assessment program. During the program participants worked in group problem-solving exercises while a staff of psychologists and line managers observed them. Afterwards participants got feedback on their performance.

    The feedback on my participant said that he was so intelligent he frequently had the right answers before the rest of the group had even defined the problem. Then the report made a statement I'll never forget. It said that his "being right was irrelevant."

How could "being right" be "irrelevant"? It was irrelevant because he could never communicate his "being right" to the other people in the group, and all the problem solutions required their cooperation. At the end of each exercise he watched the others move off in the wrong direction because they never listened to him.

Why didn't they listen? The answer was simple. He didn't listen to them. He didn't notice that they simply didn't understand him. He didn't ask questions to test what they did and did not understand about what he was saying. He didn't notice the obvious fact that he was ramming final solutions down their throats while they were still disagreeing on what the problems were. He wouldn't stand back, analyze where they were in their progress, help them diagnose, lead them through the thinking process he'd gone through in arriving at a solution, and help them contribute to and develop personal ownership in the solution.

He had plenty of clues. They asked him questions that would have shown him where they were. But he wouldn't respond at their level. He continually blocked out the data that would have told him where they were. Instead he interpreted their questions as resistance to or criticism of his ideas. When he didn't answer the questions they asked, but each time launched into another repetitive hard sell of his own final solutions, they concluded he was a little slow and not bright enough to understand them. His responses were indeed "irrelevant" to the specific questions they were asking. They began to ignore him and the more his frustration built the more he began to sound like an ineffective broken record. What a frustrating fate for the most intelligent person in the group!

This same type of frustration is common in career discussions between a manager and an employee. The manager often feels obligated (unrealistically) to tell the employee what to do. The employee disagrees but doesn't know how to express the disagreement. Sensing an undefined resistance, the manager gets frustrated and comes on with a harder and harder sell. Soon neither is listening and neither is willing to articulate the frustration their noncommunication is generating.

Fifty percent of creativity is convincing your own boss

Another example that increased my awareness of how critical communications skills are came to my attention several years ago when a study of successful executives entitled *Mobile Manager: A Study of the New Generation of Top Executives* reported that "the mobile manager knows that the better half of creativity is selling a bright idea to a supervisor."[4] There are many people with bright ideas in organizations, but not many who will tolerantly and relentlessly persist in the face of resistance to change, preoccupied management, and all the other rejections and communications barriers bright ideas are likely to encounter before they get accepted.

These persisters are the people who are most likely to get what they want in organizations—including career satisfaction—and they don't persist through stubborn repetitiveness. They persist flexibly, often quietly, and with considerable intuitive or learned awareness of the interpersonal communications process.

One of the things they tend to do regularly is anticipate potential emotional blocks, biases, preconceived notions, and other possible communications barriers to ideas they want to present; and carefully tailor their presentations to deal with these. If the presentations fail the first time, they listen carefully to find out why and, armed with these facts, redesign their communications approach to try again later.

In this and subsequent chapters we will be talking about how to develop this awareness, what it consists of, and how to use it to expand your own repertoires for persuasion in negotiating a satisfying career contract with an employer.

Awareness begins with split vision

Awareness begins with split vision. Split vision involves noticing that there are two distinct dimensions in any interpersonal communication, and learning to deal with both. These dimensions are *Content* and *Process*. I'll introduce them here the same way I introduce them when I conduct a career-planning workshop—with an exercise.[5]

Content is important (an exercise)

Early on the first morning of my workshops I ask participants to pair off with someone they've never met before.

When the pairs are formed, I ask them to take five minutes and tell each other as much as possible about themselves. This allows two and a half minutes per person.

As a reader you can simulate this by thinking about what information you'd give a total stranger if you had to communicate as much as possible about yourself in two minutes. Picture yourself in a group of strangers with no idea how your partner will be asked to use the data you present.

Take two minutes and think.

What did you say? If you're typical of our workshop participants, you gave some pretty standard, stereotyped information such as:

Name	Job Title
Age	Company or Organization
Education	Sports Preferences
Marital Status	Place of Birth

In short, you gave facts—statistics. It was probably rather safe, low-risk, standard data. You spoke in the type of categories (age, marital status, occupation) we typically use to get a fix on strangers in new situations or at cocktail parties.

For the remainder of this book, we will refer to this category of data as Content. Content is very important.

Most of our daily communication, particularly on the job, centers around Content. Content is essential, but it is inadequate by itself. It gives us only part of the data we need in dealing with any situation involving people.

Process is critical (an exercise)

After we've discussed Content, I ask people to separate back into the same pairs.

This time I tell them to take another five minutes (two and a half minutes per person) to tell each other how they "felt" during the first five-minute encounter.

This takes some explanation. People are used to being asked for Content. They respond easily and automatically.

People are not used to being asked how they feel, particularly by strangers in a public gathering.

The question of relevance arises. Who ever asks how I feel? What's that got to do with anything?

We have to repeat the question and assure people they heard correctly.

Picture yourself having to tell a stranger you've spent five minutes with how you felt during that five minutes.

Take two minutes and think what feelings you'd express.

What did you say?

If you are like our workshop participants, you said such things as—

Anxious	Suspicious	Confused	Uncertain
Tricked	Hesitant	Fearful	Exposed

In reading and thinking through this exercise alone, you are missing one critical learning experience the workshop participants get at this point. That is the unexpected experience of sharing some of your private feelings (and frustrations) with someone you've just met.

Participants find they like that experience. It's new. It's exciting, but it's also a little scary.

Again the questions "Where is all this leading?" "What does this have to do with anything?"

What indeed? How many of us on the job have strong feelings about things that we suppress? How much of our energy is devoted to this suppression, particularly if the feelings concern our personal career satisfaction or lack of it? How much anger and hostility do we suppress and blame on the manager, organization, or system that doesn't understand, perceive, or respond to these critical concerns of ours that we never find an acceptable way to communicate?

We've left Content now and moved into Process, the second, equally critical but usually overlooked dimension of interpersonal and interorganizational communications. Process is very different from Content. Content refers to the literal data that's being communicated (age, title, degree, etc.). Content is the surface, spoken communication. Content is *what* is said.

Process looks between the lines. Process refers to the too-often overlooked dynamics of the communication exchange. Process is *how* something is said—with what feelings, anxieties, fears, values, expectations, needs, and assumptions, influencing both the sender and the receiver. Process determines such things as:

- What is said and not said.

- What is heard and not heard.

- What is accepted and rejected (silently).

- What is implied and not implied.

- Whether or not any real communication takes place at all.

If the Process issues go unnoticed, unspoken, and unclarified (as they usually do in our work culture), I can never have a clear understanding with any manager or organization about pursuing my personal career goals.

When Process issues are ignored, people often talk past rather than to each other. This is what was happening in our earlier example. There being right ended up being irrelevant for the individual who looked only at the Content of his solution and ignored the Process of how and why his Content was not being accepted.

Once the ice is broken, Process issues can be fun. Early in our split vision exercise, one sharp and sensitive participant observed that: "The second five minutes was more interesting."

The group agreed. In the second five minutes they had been more authentic, more truly themselves. They had taken some risks. They had exposed themselves a little and practiced, briefly, the recovery of those Process dimensions of self we tend to lose on the job.

Once beyond the Content stereotypes they had shared mutual anxieties. They had established better relationships and, in a small way, started to build trust. They had, some of them, allowed themselves one brief moment of vulnerability. Being vulnerable had led to increased excitement, relevance, and growth.

It really was "more interesting."

Don't keep personalities out of things

Our organizational cultures are filled with people who have been taught as a matter of principle to avoid or deny the reality of Process, particularly on the job. They know, as all of us do at some level, that the Process issues are there, but they've been taught to pretend they aren't.

These people look at half a world and label their incomplete vision "Objectivity" or "Pragmatism." "Don't give me feelings," they say, "Give me facts, only facts." They are like the character Jack Webb plays on Dragnet, inhumanly nonexpressive. These people are also rather boring. They aren't much fun. They don't have much fun either. They've learned to "keep personalities out of things."

But my personality is me, everything that makes me unique and different from everyone else. If I have to leave my personality at home, it won't be surprising that I feel something important is missing or "lost" at work.

I don't leave my personality at home in situations like this, of course. Instead I carry it right with me and suppress it, or mold it out of shape to meet others' expectations. Both suppressing and molding out of shape are fatiguing endeavors. I can become so accomplished at both I forget what I'm doing, and I wonder where all that energy is going.

The culture that suppresses feelings, emotion, and Process in favor of facts ignores one critical reality. Feelings and emotions are facts. People have them. They affect people's behavior. Feelings, whether we acknowledge them or not, are just as real as any numbers that come off a computer.

Let's look at an example of how avoiding Process issues can create major problems in career planning.

The interpersonal quadrilogue[6]

A quadrilogue separates any conversation between two people into four dimensions as follows:

The Quadrilogue

Part 1 (Process)	Part 2 (Content)	Part 3 (Content)	Part 4 (Process)
My unspoken private thoughts and feelings.	My overt actions and spoken words.	Other person's overt actions and spoken words.	Other person's unspoken private thoughts and feelings.

The following quadrilogue involves communication that takes place between a boss and a subordinate.

The boss (Joe) has identified this subordinate as a top-potential employee capable of rising to high levels of broad general management. He's training the subordinate for this. He is benevolently doing all he can to provide the type of administrative and manpower management experience needed for a manager's growth.

The subordinate (Jane) is a bright, natural, highly committed technologist who wants to do research, get her Ph.D., teach, and make her mark as a technical innovator. She has no interest in administrative or managerial work.

Neither has communicated any expectations and plans to the other. Neither has asked the other. Neither is aware of what the conflict is, but both are uncomfortable. Both avoid mentioning their uncomfortableness to the other.

The boss calls Jane in to give her another of many recent administrative (management development) type assignments.

Their conversation, and examples of the four dimensions in the quadrilogue, are shown in Table 3.1.

Table 3.1   Interpersonal quadrilogue

Jane (Subordinate)		Joe (Boss)	
Private thoughts and feelings	Overt actions	Overt actions	Private thoughts and feelings
I'm really upset about these administrative assignments. ▶	Polite greeting Glum expression		
			▶ Jane looks upset. So am I. I guess we are both working too hard. ◀
		Returns polite greeting. Says: Jane, we must talk about this manpower project.	
Manpower! My test program is at a crucial point and he wants to talk manpower. I'm confused. ▶	◀		
	Suppressing her irritation, says: Joe, can the manpower thing wait? I need your reaction to some test data.		
			▶ Test data! Here I am trying to get her promoted and she wants

Table 3.1 *Continued*

Jane (Subordinate)		Joe (Boss)	
Private thoughts and feelings	Overt actions	Overt actions	Private thoughts and feelings
			to talk test data. Can't she see how important this is to her career! I'm confused. ◄
		Masking irritation, says: Jane, I'm sure you can work the test data, but right now this manpower thing is important.	
Damn! Can't he see this manpower assignment is a thorn in my side. I must remain calm. ◄	O.K., Joe, if you insist ►		Dammit! If I insist. How can she be so blind? Why is she trying to bait me? I must remain calm. ◄
		Jane, I know you are deep into the project, but the test data must wait.	
It is hard to believe but I guess he just doesn't care about my work. ◄	O.K., Joe, I'll let it wait. ►		I'm relieved. I'll try to explain why this is so important to her. ◄
		Jane, I'm glad you understand.	

Does Jane really understand?

In masking their true concerns and in ignoring the issue of their mutual uncomfortableness, the data needed to "understand" has been buried. Let's examine the buried data in Table 3.2.

Table 3.2   Process issues avoided

Jane	Process issues	Boss
1. High value placed upon achievement as a technical specialist	Values	1. High value placed upon advancement in engineering management
2. Expects rewards in terms of professional recognition	Expectations	2. Expects rewards in terms of promotion, pay, status, management authority
3. Getting sidetracked into nontechnical work	Fears	3. Getting passed over for promotion
4. To be a full professor at M.I.T.	Goals	4. To be general manager
5. To be seen as a leader in her technical field	Needs	5. To be seen as an outstanding technical manager
6. Management work is a noncreative dead end	Assumptions	6. Management of technically competent people is a real challenge
7. Center around being unable to generate creative solutions to technical problems	Anxieties	7. Center around being rejected by power figures in the company

Table 3.2 shows some of the Process issues avoided in the quadrilogue conversation.

There is no reason why Jane should have the same values, expectations, and goals as her boss. Yet both are consuming valuable energy avoiding the differences. Certainly both sense that there is a serious and growing breakdown in their communication. Still neither is willing to articulate what he or she senses. They both avoid the Process issues of communications breakdown and disagreement on goal priority, sticking instead doggedly and unproductively to the Content issue of administrative assignments.

To evaluate the pragmatism of avoiding the Process issues ask yourself the following questions.

- How productive was the conversation?

- How much longer (weeks—months—years) might it continue to go on unproductively?

- What is the cost in dollars? These are obviously two well-paid talents. How much of their paid for creative time and energies are being dissipated suppressing or fighting the internal frustrations this brand of noncommunication generates?

Before long, Jane, a valuable talent, will very likely leave in frustration. Replacing her with a recruiting, hiring, moving in, and orientation training program will be expensive. Costly managerial time will be devoted to this.

They did indeed succeed in keeping feelings, emotions, and personalities out of their overt communications. Neither revealed his or her uncomfortableness, anxieties, or frustrations. They maintained their surface cool and remained stoic.

Obviously this is neither pragmatic nor good for the individuals involved.

But it isn't obvious.

The costs of ignoring Process are subtle, hidden, and unnoticed. Deadly as they are, they elude management awareness and never show up on the balance sheet.

The costs of ignoring Process in strategizing our own careers tend to stay hidden and unnoticed too. They pop up in strange places like pharmacy bills for antacids or tranquilizers, in tension at home, in liquor bills, and in raises that slow down or stop coming altogether.

How to deal with process

Dealing effectively in the Process dimensions requires personal introspection to identify what I am feeling and what it is I am reacting to in a given situation.

It also requires a willingness to share—disclose—the results of my introspection to the other person. Introspection without sharing tends to become increasingly autistic and distorted.

Sharing involves:

- *Owning Up.* Noticing (not suppressing) my feelings, anxieties, needs, and values. Accepting them as mine and finding effective ways to communicate them when they are factors in the situation at hand.

- *Helping Others to Own Up and Be Open.*   Actively seeking to understand and listen to the feelings, anxieties, needs, and values of others, particularly when they are different from mine. Setting the example by being open myself helps a lot in this.

- *Interpersonal Competence.*   Becoming aware of interpersonal dynamics. Developing a practical set of diagnostic tools for use in assessing what's really going on in the Process dimensions (within me and with other people); and expanding my repertoire of interpersonal communications techniques so I can deal effectively with Process issues, even when working with people who don't understand Process themselves.

Too often we assume other people share our own feelings and values when they don't, or we assume they know what our own feelings and values are when we have never communicated them.

Jane's boss in the quadrilogue assumed she wanted to be a manager. There are several reasons Jane might have been keeping her silence. She might have assumed her boss knew she didn't want to be a manager. She might, on the other hand, have been afraid for her boss to find out she didn't want to be a manager because she:

- assumed telling him would hurt his feelings (I don't want to be like you, Daddy).

- assumed telling him would anger him (he was already angry).

- assumed telling him would make him think less of her (if you don't have the aggressiveness to want management you're dead in this company).

In reality, the truth would probably have been far less likely to anger the boss or endanger Jane's position than the repeated impasses they were experiencing over the administrative assignments.

We tend to assume a lot in the Process dimensions of interpersonal communications. The biggest assumption in organizations seems to be that we are not allowed to discuss or disclose Process data at all. "You're supposed to grin and bear it around here."

When I sense communications are breaking down and introspection tells me the problem is probably a Process issue, the simplest way to find out and break the impasse is to ask a Process question.

It isn't very difficult to do this, and the other person is frequently relieved that someone broke the ice.

It didn't take much introspection for both Jane and Joe to know the situation between them was becoming uncomfortable and repetitive. They were both actively trying to read each other's minds and assuming the worst. Jane was thinking, "I guess he just doesn't care about my work," and Joe was thinking, "How can she be so blind? Why is she trying to bait me?"

Suppose Joe had decided to own up to his feelings by saying, "Jane, I'm feeling confused and uncomfortable about our communications lately. Somehow they're breaking down. Do you feel it too? Is there something about these assignments that's bothering you?" Chances are whole new dimensions of Process data would have entered the conversation to help clear things up.

If Joe hadn't taken the initiative, Jane might have said something like "Joe, is there something I'm doing that's annoying you lately? I can sense you getting angry and frankly that's a little scary. I don't want to let you down on the test program, and I'm feeling overwhelmed with these administrative assignments. Can we talk about it?"

If Joe had responded angrily to Jane's overture, Jane still would have been better off for knowing what Joe thought and why he was giving her administrative assignments. Joe was angry anyway, even though he wasn't expressing it. Some temporary anger would have been a small price for clearing up the question of career goals and getting Jane back on track with assignments that were in line with her values.

Even in the very improbable event that Joe remained permanently angry and continued to insist Jane take managerial assignments, Jane would have been better off for knowing where Joe stood. Knowing Joe's feelings and expectations, Jane could have retreated and quietly begun a search for new employment somewhere where she could pursue her own goals.

The worst possible outcome would have been for both to remain silent permanently and have Jane give up her technical goals to satisfy the system (or Joe) and become a manager.

Someone has to establish the norm for sharing Process information. Almost always the other person responds in kind, grateful for the chance.

If Jane and Joe had productively diagnosed the process of how their communications were breaking down, they could have then negotiated a new, more reality-oriented career contract for Jane.

Contracts are addressed in the next chapter.

Career contract realities 4

Contracts are based on expectations

When I speak of career contracts between individuals and organizations, I'm not suggesting each employee needs a detailed legal document presided over by a lawyer. I refer rather to the too-often unarticulated psychological contract between an employee and an employer; to the frequently implied but seldom defined set of mutual expectations that arise concerning who can be relied on to do what, and when, to further the mutual interests of both the individual and the organization. The myths discussed in an earlier chapter are examples of how dangerous and misleading any ill-defined expectations can be, particularly when they imply that an employee can rely on an organization to do more than the organization can realistically promise.

Expectations must be articulated

If they are to form the base for a clear contract, expectations must be articulated, realistic, and understood by all concerned. Understanding who is expected to do what is critical to the success of any activity, even something as apparently passive as reading a book or hearing a lecture.

For instance, what is your contract with me, as you read this book? It shouldn't be one-sided. Think about it. You expect me to write something that is informative and useful. What do you expect of yourself? Shouldn't you contribute too? I'll illustrate this with an exercise.

Expectations (an exercise)[7]

Before reading further, sit back quietly and get as comfortable as you can. Rid your mind of distractions. Think about what you are feeling and wanting right now.

Ask yourself the following questions. Close your eyes, and think quietly about the answer after reading each question.

1. What do you really want to get out of reading this book? What would the best of all outcomes be for you personally?

2. What can you do personally to make sure this happens? What actions, energy, or attitude can you personally contribute as opposed to remaining passive and expecting the book to do it alone?

3. Based on past experiences (books, workshops, discussions, abortive career-planning attempts), what can you do personally to foul it up? What are you likely to think, assume, or do to make certain your best of all outcomes doesn't happen? Relax and be honest. You don't have to show this to anyone.

4. Attach a feeling to this, a one-word feeling (angry, hostile, disappointed, confused, fearful, etc.) that usually comes to you when your hoped for expectations aren't met. This will probably be a very familiar feeling you experience often. Remember it. This feeling can become a built-in warning signal that you need to make a contract with yourself for change.

5. What can you do to prevent the foul-up? How can you learn from past experience? How can you avoid things you might do to prevent your best possible outcome? What can you do differently this time to help you get what you want?

6. Looking at your answers to these questions, how can you now turn getting what you want in the book and in life into an exciting, energy-generating challenge?

Begin the rest of your life with a challenge

The above exercise makes several useful points at the beginning of a career-planning workshop. It is a new experience for most people to begin a workshop (or a book) by being challenged. Unexpectedly they have to look at themselves, to make a commitment to themselves about what they personally will do to make the experience meaningful for them. They have to admit there are ways they might prevent themselves from realizing their expectations and look at ways they can avoid that.

Most of us begin a lecture, book, or workshop with a passive "show-me" attitude. We assume the detached role of critic. We expect to be entertained or improved. The burden and responsibility for results is on the teacher or author.

Being challenged is important. I should begin planning the rest of my life by being challenged. I should be very personally committed to getting desired results. It is my life.

Most of us enter an organization with a "tell-me" attitude concerning our careers. Tell me what to do. I'll do it. I expect you to make certain it's worth my while. "Show me" the way. I'll follow and work hard. If it doesn't lead to my satisfaction, the "system" went wrong. The "system" didn't strategize my career correctly.

It's an unspoken, unspecified contract. When we really think about it, we know it's a naive, unreal contract. But how often do we take time to think about it?

It's safe to blame the "system." Systems are always imperfect. No one will contradict us on this. Systems are nonpersonal "its."

Unspecified contracts with "its" give me a safe outlet for blame, but they don't make me feel much better if I'm not getting what I want. It is more productive and fun to negotiate specific contracts that get me what I want in workshops, and in life.

There are two types of contracts involved in the process of planning my career. These are:

- contracts I make with myself to do specific things that are required to meet my career goals.

- contracts I make with other people when meeting my goals requires cooperative action with someone else.

Contracts with organizations are the second type. They involve other people.

Contracts with an organization

In planning the rest of my career in an organization I should carefully identify:

- what I need to contribute.

- what my supervisor can be expected to contribute.

- what the organization can be expected to contribute.

- what the ground rules are going to be.

Career planning and contracting within an organization are forms of cooperative problem solving.

Problem solving without valid data is an exercise in frustration. The Process issues of what I want, need, expect, and value are valid data in any career-planning contract negotiations with my superiors.

Negotiating effectively to include these issues in a contract with an employer requires that I first define them for myself. I must decide what I really want for me (as distinct from what my boss, the organization, or my peers think I should want) before I can begin negotiating to get what I want.

The values I want to realize in life along with the personal interests, skills, and abilities I want to pursue on the job become my criteria for looking behind doors and focusing on a specific career path. Pursuing a career that meets my unique personal criteria is success for me. I should contract for this.

An organization can try to create a proper climate and provide tools and techniques to help me develop my criteria; but no superior or personnel department can ethically tell me what I should want (though many try and, unfortunately, many people listen).

The organization can help me collect data to decide which career paths meet my criteria. The organization can make incumbents and experts in different career paths available to give me information. The organization can help me become aware of openings that may meet my criteria (if I identify and communicate them).

In short, the organization can and should supply information and data to help me decide, but I must learn to ask for this data.

The organization can answer questions. I must learn to develop and ask questions to generate specific data that's relevant to my unique decisions. Organizations don't have ESP.

Once I have defined the "what," the organization can assist on the "how" (training programs, tuition refund, job opportunities, location choices). The possibilities are endless. I must sort out and select those which are uniquely relevant to me. Otherwise I may spend years at a "which door" impasse.

The supermarket supplies an enormous variety of foods. The supermarket does not design my diet, force feed me, determine whether I'm to be fat or thin, low or high in cholesterol. I do that. The supermarket may try to program what I eat through aggressive advertising. If I have any sense, I ignore the advertising and decide for myself.

If I use my brain to identify and develop some skills of value, organizations can become my job supermarkets. If I get really good at something and one organization doesn't carry my preferred job brand, there are other organizations, none of which have enough really good people. I can shop.

The foregoing is so obvious it may sound condescending, even trite.

As you read on, however, you may discover your part of the career-planning contract isn't obvious at all. Avoiding tough decisions on contradictory values (e.g., location versus opportunity) may have you at a career impasse. You may be avoiding the decision so skillfully you aren't even aware of the conflict or the impasse. You may require a contract with yourself to break through the impasse and get your life moving again.

Contracts with myself

I believe organizations have a clear obligation to help educate employees on how to define their own criteria for success and select career paths that meet these criteria. The reality is, however, that most organizations don't do this very well yet.

The reality is that most people who have succeeded to date in getting what they want out of a career have had to find ways to do it without any organization's help. In my opinion this includes the presidents of most companies. They got there despite the systems; or they looked at the systems' realities and found ways to manipulate them to their personal advantage. Intuitively, they realized they couldn't wait or depend on any system. They took charge, made a contract with themselves, and acted.

Making a contract with myself to get my life moving in directions I want to go begins with accepting the fact that I am a prime contributor to just about everything that happens to me. Good things seldom happen without my taking some action to make them happen.

Likewise (aside from earthquakes, disease, or other dramatic acts of God), I am usually an active contributor when things don't go my way. If I'm failing to meet one of my important career goals and I think about the facts objectively, I'll usually discover I am influencing the situation. There are many ways I can do this. For example:

Not doing something that's required of me to meet the goal. I may not be pursuing the needed training (full time or after hours) to qualify for something I want to do; not investigating what self-generated action steps are required to get what I want (how did people who hold these jobs qualify themselves?); or not taking the first known action step required (asking my boss about a new assignment) for fear of failure or rejection. I may simply not be defining what I want even to myself.

Meeting a contradictory goal that's more important to me, and not admitting to myself that I've actually made the tradeoff. Maintaining my current salary level and life-style may really be more important to me than that lower paying social-service job I'd like to take. I can't have both and I've really made the choice, but I won't accept it. Because I feel guilty, I vacillate, punish myself by not enjoying the money, agonize in bogus indecision, and complain that social-service people should make more money.* As a result, even though I've made the trade-off, I end up getting no personal satisfaction from either value (money or social service). I may have decided that maintaining my current part-time church work is more important to me than the prestige and new challenges I'd get in a better job that would require too much travel to continue my outside activities. If so, I hope I can relax and enjoy that as my unique and very authentic version of success. Otherwise, again, I end up getting no satisfaction from either value.

Actively doing something that is preventing me from meeting my goal. For fear of mistakes and possible failure, I may be refusing to delegate—making all the decisions myself, discounting my subordinates' abilities, and working long hours to do their work for them. That pattern will make it difficult for me to meet a goal of assuming a higher-level managerial job with additional responsibility and more subordinates to think for. This is a frequent self-defeating career pattern in industry. When people like this

---

* It may be true that social-service people should make more money. However, if I don't plan to work actively at getting them more money (another value trade-off on how I'll spend my time) there is nothing to be gained and much to be lost by keeping myself agitated over the subject.

get passed over for promotion, they feel very persecuted because they work so hard and it isn't recognized.

Once I learn to notice what I am doing—or not doing—to help or hinder my career progress, I can develop a very conscious contract with myself to improve things. I can decide what has to be done, in what sequence, and assume ongoing personal responsibility for assuring things happen as planned. I can review my contract periodically and measure progress.

Essential contract ingredients

The specifics of contracts like this will differ with each personal goal. Generically, ingredients essential to any contract with myself for assuring my on-the-job growth and satisfactions would include:

Value analysis—Identifying my most important values (money, location, time with family, managing others, being an individual expert, etc.); rank-ordering them, and deciding which I'll trade off if faced with a contradiction (e.g., the job I want not being available in the location I want). Many people keep themselves in a state of continual agitation by refusing to face these decisions.

Establishing job-content objectives—Identifying what specific combination of muscles (intellectual, interpersonal, technical, physical, artistic, mathematical, etc.) I want to be developing and exercising in my future on-the-job activities. These objectives become my criteria for judging the content of potential future jobs. If a potential opening involves doing a lot of financial or technical analysis by myself with no opportunity for interacting with others, and interacting with others is important to me, I will avoid that job even if it's a promotion. I can't look behind doors effectively until I have some standard to use for judging whether or not what I find is for me.

Collecting real (not stereotyped) data to determine what types of jobs really meet my personal content criteria—I can't decide whether or not I want to be a marketing manager, a general manager, or a college professor until I've talked to several people who have done these things and found out specifically how they spend their day. I need data to measure against my content criteria. This sounds obvious but I deal daily with grown-ups, some at very high levels, who have never collected this type of data for themselves. Many are beating themselves to death because they are bored with what they are doing and can't decide where they want to go next. Who can decide with no data, or with superficial speculations about what other people do, or with stereotyped position-guide descriptions? These same people wouldn't make business decisions with such limited data. It's only their lives they have no time for.

Establishing an objective and a plan—Identifying a specific goal, one that represents the best possible match up to muscles I want to exercise and dimensions along which I want to grow. This requires collecting data to find out precisely what it takes to get there, matching that data to my current qualifications, and generating next job options to fill in the gaps.

Negotiating continuously—Maintaining an ongoing series of formal and informal negotiations between me and my organization on a quid pro quo basis so that I can contribute to organization goals and at the same time continue to grow toward my own goals on some reasonable timetable. Our interviews have shown successful people seldom wait for the organization to suggest job changes to them. They tend to be very squeaky wheels about getting what they want. If a job gets tiresome or they have outgrown it, they find a way to change without waiting to be asked.

Developing interpersonal competence—Few people are intuitive Process experts. Most successful people have worked hard and consciously at developing their persuasive skills and interpersonal techniques. Lack of interpersonal competence is a major barrier (in my opinion *the* major barrier) to negotiating self-fulfilling and growth-oriented work in an organizational environment.

Updating regularly—A good career (or life) plan involves a series of conscious decisions over time. It is a flexible, rolling forecast that I update regularly to incorporate such things as new data assimilated, temporary setbacks, and new value insights. Planning to get what I want is not a one-shot effort.

Ongoing reality testing—Checking out my career strategies by continuously collecting data to verify or disprove their effectiveness from all sources available. Data sources would include peers, appropriate management figures, and (above all) experts in my fields of interest. Dialogue with others is essential if I want to keep my feet on the ground and avoid nonproductive daydreaming. The relevant others should consist primarily of people who have successfully performed in the type of work I aspire to do. Obviously, I don't expect anyone I talk with to tell me what to do. (They will probably all disagree on that anyway.) I talk to others to collect specific data that will help *me* decide and strategize what *I* want to do.

On first glance, an approach like the above may look pretty time-consuming, but it doesn't have to be. Done right, it can end up being time-conserving.

There is a common misconception that the only way people can achieve career goals is to devote so much time and energy to them that all other values are traded off. This is not necessarily so. Some achieve career goals that way. Others focus their energies in an intelligent, data-based fashion that enables them to concentrate on high-impact (as opposed to make-work) efforts and leaves plenty of time for other things.

With better focus, you may discover you can achieve more that is relevant to you with significantly less effort than you are expending now. You may be wasting a great deal of energy and time on nonproductive activities for lack of goal focus. Many people are dissipating enormous amounts of nonproductive energy in coping with anxieties generated by lack of personal goal clarity.

A clear goal conserves energy

Goal clarity and motivation are two key interrelating variables in the process of getting what I want on the job. If we think in terms of an economy of energy model, goal clarity and motivation interact to influence how effectively we generate and use energy.

Fuzzy or ill-defined goals don't invite much self-generated motivation to achieve them. With unclear goals, energy is dissipated on confusion and anxiety. By clarifying goals I can liberate this dissipated energy and make it available for productive achievement. Goal clarity makes it possible to focus my energies on activities that are directly relevant to accomplishing career goals. With focus, I can work smarter instead of longer.

Hopefully, you are already in the position of having clear goals and active self-fulfilling programs for achieving them. It is my observation, however, that relatively few people working in large impersonal organizations (even at very high levels) are already in that position. The most noticeable symptom that all is not well is anxiety.

When to contract for change

If anxiety is the symptom, anxiety is also the clue. Anxiety is my own, internal, automatic-warning signal that all is not right and it's time for a contract with myself to analyze why and make a course correction. In this sense, anxiety can be a positive, beneficial experience.

Most of us try to suppress anxiety. We deny it, blot it out, or try to force it to go away. We see it as a negative reflection on our worth, a sign that something is wrong with us.

Everyone has anxieties. Anxiety doesn't necessarily mean something is wrong with us. It's often merely a signal that something may be wrong in our lives, or perhaps simply that something might be better.

Anxiety can be a very positive motivator for change. Many of the world's most significant accomplishments would never have happened without people getting anxious about the way things were to the point where they wanted to improve them.

We should not suppress anxiety. It's more productive to let ourselves experience it and get in touch with what's causing it. We should look for what it is we are reacting to in the situation, and for what it is we ourselves are doing, or not doing, to maintain the difficulty.

Dealing with the known is easier than suppressing the unknown, and it's less fatiguing. When we know what's causing anxiety we can develop a plan for improving things. If we've made a mistake, we can learn from it and begin corrective action. All of us make a lot of mistakes. That's also a natural trait that needn't be blotted out.

Action is the prescription for a building anxiety, and past mistakes are the basic building blocks for future growth.

Anxiety may mean I've succeeded

There is a form of anxiety common in our work lives that has nothing to do with mistakes. It has to do with plateaus and boredom.

In graphing my own life to date on age versus growth and satisfaction, I found a clear cyclical pattern (see Fig. 4.1). Each period of

Fig. 4.1   Sample life graphic (Anxiety is the basic motivator of change and growth.) (This figure is a modification of a similar life line graph developed by Dr. Herbert A. Shepard. It is used by permission of Dr. Shepard.)

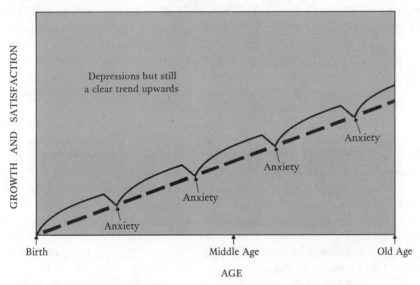

Don't suppress anxiety. Use it to your advantage. Let anxiety be your alert signal. Get in touch with it. Feel it, look for the cause, and develop a plan of corrective action.

Let boredom turn on your search mechanism for what it is you want to do more than what you are doing. Then reach out and find it.

excitement, energy, and growth was followed by a leveling off and then a plateau. The plateau meant I had mastered what there was to learn in a given job or challenge and my learning had stopped. I rested on the plateau for a while and then went into a satisfaction slump. I got bored, tired, and anxious. When the slump dropped low enough that I became acutely uncomfortable, this roused me enough that I forced myself into a new job or situation where I could start up the growth and learning curve again.

This graph gave me new perceptions and insights. Before, I always got depressed when I felt anxious or bored. I assumed all my anxieties were signs I had taken a wrong turn, failed, or been wasting my life on the wrong thing. When I felt this way I fought change. I felt acknowledging I needed change was acknowledging failure.

The graph gave a different perspective. It showed anxiety and boredom could be signs I had succeeded; signs I had mastered something and was ready to build on that, to move on to a new and higher plateau. Somehow, to me at least, that is what life in this world is about—overcoming barriers, mastering things, growing, and moving on to new plateaus. That ties in with what I've been taught in most of my religious training also. I was glad to see these different areas of my life beginning to integrate and coalesce. I felt good about it.

Anxiety isn't quite so scary anymore. It's another "on" button for forward movement and growth.

If you are reading through this book now with no desire to use its techniques for changing anything, one reason may be that you are in the middle of a satisfying growth curve—or resting on a plateau consolidating your energies for the next climb.

When you finish the book, keep it on your shelf. When (and if) you start on the down slope, get it out again.

If you are avoiding thinking about change for fear that would be acknowledging past mistakes, stop doing that. Only losers believe they can't make mistakes. Winners expect to make lots of mistakes, learn from them, and move on.

There may not be any mistakes involved at all. You may simply be at the end of a firm and successfully built plateau. That's a strong signal you're ready to look higher.

Those of us with families and financial obligations can't relieve anxiety by quitting our jobs tomorrow and taking up fishing in Hawaii or skiing in the Yukon. Nevertheless, we can almost always, at any age and without jeopardizing our incomes, find ways to negotiate for new challenges and growth in our current situations, on and off the job. Also, most of us, if we sit down, use our brains, and make a contract with ourselves to develop a strategy, can develop many more options than we realize for maintaining our income and still finding more exciting work (inside and outside our current organizations).

Often when we feel anxiety and the need for a career change, we seek out someone who can serve as a career counselor to help us generate new action plans. This can be very beneficial when approached realistically, and a real pitfall if approached naively. Before we talk to a counselor, we should look carefully at the realities of what career counselors can and cannot be expected to contribute.

Career
counseling
realities 5

Counselors play a limited role

What can I realistically expect from career counselors? What should their role really be? What responsibilities can I expect them to assume in my contract with an organization?

We talked about things the manager or personnel department can't do (e.g., decide my values for me). What can they do to help when I go to them for counseling?

My manager and personnel representative can help me obtain required data about open jobs in the organization. They can help me investigate the content and skill requirements of those jobs to which I may aspire. On the latter, hopefully, they will help me schedule data-collecting interviews with people who are now performing or have actually performed the jobs in question. Telephones can be useful for conducting these data-collecting interviews with people at other geographic locations, but face-to-face meetings are preferable.

Aside from helping me obtain data to answer specific questions that I have generated, the most helpful thing my manager and personnel specialist can do for me as counselors is serve as good listeners and sounding boards.

One of the best ways to understand the realities—and the limitations—of a counselor's role is to experience it by doing some practice counseling. When I conduct a career-planning workshop I have the participants break up into groups and rotate roles (counselors and counselees).[8] Those being counseled describe what they feel have been their most rewarding accomplishments to date in life. The others serve as career counselors and facilitators helping the counselees explore the nuances of meaning the accomplishments had for them.

This switching of roles serves two purposes. The people being counseled get to explore their accomplishments. This helps them begin to tune in on what kind of things they like to do most. The people serving as counselors get practice at sitting on the manager or personnel consultant's side of the table. They get some reality orientation on what any career counselor can and cannot be expected to do.

Counseling do's and don'ts

I establish ground rules for the career counselors. I tell them their role is to listen attentively and help the counselees explore the meaning of the accomplishments for them. I explain that career counselors *do* help individuals explore their career preferences by:

- drawing them out,
- reflecting,
- clarifying,
- summarizing,
- encouraging, and
- accepting.

A career counselor can serve as a mirror to help people define and understand their personal values. On the other hand, career counselors *do not:*

- evaluate me or tell me what I am or am not capable of doing (I might surprise them),*
- tell me what I should do,
- moralize (tell me my values or goals are good or bad),
- tell me what my motives are (they can't read minds), or
- try to persuade me to adopt a different point of view.

---

* Various forms of psychological testing can give me some useful data or guidelines, but even these are fallible and it takes a real professional in the behavioral sciences to help me interpret them. One of the first things a real professional always does is point out the tests' fallibilities.

Career counselors are ineffective if they try to dictate, judge, or decide the other person's values—or if they try to sell the other person on their own (career counselors') values. This type of behavior discounts the autonomy and potency of the individuals being counseled. This type of behavior is also taking on themselves (as counselors) a heavy, unreal burden of responsibility for other people's decisions and lives. If counselors take on that kind of responsibility for many other people (even if it's just in the counselors' own minds), that soon becomes a very heavy load that oppresses their own lives.

These are new concepts to people accustomed to visiting a manager or counselor for the purpose of being told what to do.

So far, none of our participants has disagreed with what these concepts say about how anyone can and cannot be expected to contribute toward helping someone else plan his or her job satisfactions.

Even a performance appraisal is fallible opinion

One of the real dangers of combined organizational performance appraisal and counseling programs that ask supervisors to predict how far an employee will go is that the employee might believe the prediction. People can give me their fallible opinions, but no one is capable of telling me what I am or am not capable of doing.

I once did a chronological study of past appraisals on several people who had achieved high-level general-management jobs in a large company. I found an interesting trend. Almost without exception, one or more past managers of these people had stated categorically that the individual did not have the capability to become a general manager.

I don't know what conclusion to draw from this. Clearly, the appraising managers had been proved wrong. Clearly, the successful general managers had ignored or defied the predictions. Possibly the prediction itself was one of the things that challenged some to face their mistakes and learn from them.

The only message in the story is that people should take a critical look at anything a manager or career counselor tells them about their future. People being counseled are wise to use their own brains to sort out the facts they can use as clues to where they need to improve and filter out the errors, ignorances, and biases of the counselors advising them.

Counselors should not make predictions on things that are beyond their abilities to judge. Counselors can give clients their own fallible observations, feelings, reactions, and opinions as just that—fallible. Counselors should not pontificate or judge themselves by whether or not clients accept their opinions. If it becomes too important for a counselor to convince a client of something, the counselor will begin overstating and overselling.

As an antidote to inappropriate counseling, when any authority figure is counseling you, keep your antennae on and your brain tuned in. Notice if your counselors fall into the various counseling traps (or errors) described above. Filter what they say accordingly.

There are some who feel strongly that a manager should tell an employee when he or she has peaked out. I don't know what "peaked out" really means, and I don't see how any manager can know. As a manager, the best I can tell a nonperforming employee is precisely and specifically where his or her performance is not meeting my expectations (three reports were missed, the data on project X was incomplete, etc.). I can also say that in the current environment, working for me, he or she is not going to be promoted. The problem might be the employee or me, or the chemistry between us. The same employee may go to another company or field of work (or even just to another manager) and start a whole new growth career that passes me by. I've seen it happen.

References

Part 1

Chapter 1

1. From Eric Berne, *What Do You Say After You Say Hello?* (New York: Grove Press, 1972), p. 148. Reprinted with permission.

Chapter 2

2. From Charles A. Reich, *The Greening of America* (New York: Bantam Books, 1971), p. 402. Reprinted by permission of Random House, Inc.

3. Ibid., p. 402.

Chapter 3

4. From Eugene E. Jennings, *The Mobile Manager, A Study of the New Generation of Top Executives,* Bureau of Industrial Relations, Graduate School of Business Administration, The University of Michigan, 1967, p. 17. Reprinted with permission.

5. The *Split Vision* exercise was suggested by Neale Clapp of Block Petrella Associates, Plainfield, N.J.

6. The *Interpersonal Quadrilogue* example was developed by Tony Petrella of Block Petrella Associates, Plainfield, N.J.

Chapter 4

7. The *Expectations* exercise was developed by Barton Knapp and Marta Vago, and presented at a meeting of the Philadelphia Transactional Analysis Seminar.

Chapter 5

8. The basic approach for the *Career Counseling* exercise was suggested by Mike Hill of Block Petrella Associates, Plainfield, N.J.

Finding the drummer

Part 2

Whose expectations do I meet?

If I march to my own drum, how do I find the drummer? Where do I listen for the beat?

Sorting
the voices   6

It isn't easy

Separating myths from realities, dealing with the Process dimensions of communication, learning to operate autonomously with managers and counselors, and negotiating clear psychological contracts with the organization and myself to get what I want are all fundamental building blocks for effective career planning.

Each of these building blocks, of course, is a means to the more important end goal of getting what I want. To succeed at getting what I want I must, as we said earlier, know what I want. Important as this is, it is often the most frustratingly elusive building block of career planning. Too many of us have been taught to suppress what we want and instead concentrate on meeting other people's expectations. In doing this we end up spending most of our time marching to other people's drums. How do I change this and begin marching to my own drum?

It isn't easy. I must first locate the drummer and learn to hear the beat. This requires considerable effort and concentration. There are so many distractions.

The drummer is me

The drummer of course is me—that inner core that represents my true self—the reality behind the many roles I play. The drummer knows what *I* really want. To talk to the drummer, however, I must be certain I really know who I am. That isn't always as clear as I might think.

Which role?

Who I am is an even more fundamental question than what I want. I must get in touch and maintain solid contact with who I am before I can be certain I'm asking the right person what I want.

Unfortunately, who I am appears to change frequently depending on what external source is making demands. Each makes different demands and I adapt myself accordingly.

As a child, I may decide to be one thing to Daddy who wants a brave little scout; another to Mommy who wants a cuddly little child; another to an intimidating teacher who demands "perfectly clear and neat reports"; and still another to my Tom Sawyer-like peers who are impressed by kids who act tough, play ball well, and salt their conversations with a few dirty words. I learn to play many different roles, and I have to keep different people's contradictory expectations separated in my head. Mommy doesn't like dirty words and the teacher frowns on acting tough.

This splitting of self into different roles becomes more complex as I grow older. Very different demands are made on me by my boss, my subordinates, my mate, my children, and my different social friends. If I'm in Sales, I become adept at subtly switching roles to meet the unique expectations of each different customer.

This isn't all bad, but it does get confusing; and I get too good at it. Too often, unconsciously, I become so external demand-oriented that I lose "me" and discount my personal desires somewhere in the confusion.

Somehow I have to stay aware of what's going on in all these different roles and keep them integrated to maintain the essential me. I must sort out these many voices and expectations racing around inside my head and keep track of which (if any) represent me.

Most of us don't do this very well. Most of us, most of the time, are not at all clearly in contact with whose demands we are really meeting as we maintain our hectic pace, rushing through life carrying a much larger load of demands than we can ever satisfy.

Most of us don't find time to sort out all the demanding voices inside our heads. This leads to a self-defeating and self-alienating circular habit pattern. I don't have time because there are so many demands on me; and there are so many demands on me because I don't have time to sort them out and focus on essentials.

Separating the past from the present

Eric Berne and his followers, who are still developing his Transactional Analysis theories, have found after working with thousands of people that many of the demands we react to in our daily lives are archaic. They represent voices or situations from the past that are no longer relevant or required by the realities of our lives and jobs today.

I may be still pleasing the teacher by preparing too many overly detailed and typed "perfectly clear" reports when a few handwritten notes or phone calls would suffice nicely. I've seen this often in organizations when the recipients, usually superiors, would be grateful for a more concise approach. They would like to cut down on their own reading time, but some "be polite and don't hurt people's feelings" voice from their past prevents them from articulating their feelings.

If I can sort these archaic demands—if I can consciously eliminate those no longer relevant requirements of the past that I am still meeting today—I can liberate more time for the relevant values of today.

Transactional Analysis techniques (T.A.) are the best I've found for identifying archaic expectations and learning to stop responding to them. Understanding T.A. will make techniques we describe in later chapters (for identifying and getting what I want) more meaningful to you. For that reason I'll present a brief overview here before we move into those chapters.

To begin, what is there about me that makes me so responsive to others?

Why I respond to others' demands

Years ago a doctor named Spitz discovered that infants left too much alone in the impersonal care of institutions died. All their physical needs such as food, warmth, and dry clothing had been met. They had no organic ills, and still they died. Doctors called this "infant marasmus."[1]

Spitz discovered a fundamental fact about human nature: all people need to be noticed; we need to be touched; we have a basic stimulus hunger.

We stimulate infants physically. The institutionalized infants had not been fondled, played with, held, or talked to enough while they were being fed. Because no one had time to recognize their existence in any personalized way, they eventually ceased to recognize it themselves.

Eric Berne said we recognize each other with "strokes."[2] Strokes are a form of special stimulation which one person gives another. Strokes are essential to life as a means of fulfilling our basic stimulus hunger. Without strokes our spinal cords "shrivel up"[3] like the infants' did.

We never lose our need for strokes, but we expand our ways of receiving them as we grow older. Physical stimulus hunger expands to include "recognition hunger."[4] By extension, "any act implying recognition of another's presence"[5] becomes a stroke.

Strokes can be positive, negative, or conditional. They are essential to life as the "fundamental unit of social action."[6]

Examples of positive strokes on the job would be praise, a promotion, or a nod of approval for a presentation well given. Examples off the job would be a parental hug or simply the glances of recognition two friends exchange in passing on the street.

Examples of negative strokes on the job would be no raise, a reprimand, or being taken off the participant list for a critical meeting. Off-the-job examples would be a parental slap or physical punishment for mistakes.

Conditional strokes are strokes withheld until certain specified conditions are met:

- I get a raise *if* I do what I am told.

- I get the new contract *if* I perform satisfactorily on the old one.

- The children get dessert *if* they eat dinner.

- The children get love *if* they follow their parents' rules.

Unconditional positive strokes are the best. "I respect you for being you. You don't have to do anything to prove your worth to me."

If I can't get positive strokes, negative strokes are better than no strokes at all. At least I'm noticed. Who wants to shrivel up? I can always find ways to get negative strokes. The unnoticed child can spill the milk or start a fight. The bypassed executive who is suffering from job marasmas in a nonjob can create unnecessary studies and find ways to bother people by taking up their time in nonproductive ways.

From the beginning, I respond to other people's demands so that they will respond to my demands, my personal need for strokes and recognition.

Early in life I develop habit patterns around what type of strokes I set out to get and how I go about getting them.

If my parents give me a lot of positive strokes from the beginning, I develop a pretty good opinion of myself. I learn to expect positive strokes, and I develop positive behavior patterns that elicit them. When there is no one around, I learn to think positively about myself and give myself positive strokes.

If my parents ignored me much of the time and behaving positively didn't gain their attention, I soon learned negative behavior patterns that would elicit negative strokes. Perhaps I learned to get attention by doing things that annoyed people and forced them to give me at least the recognition of negative strokes. After years of maintaining my survival (fulfilling my stimulus hunger) on negative strokes, I habitually solicit negative strokes from people because I haven't learned to solicit positive strokes. I may also have never learned I deserve positive strokes. When no one else is around I pull negative strokes out of my past experience and tell myself I'm a loser.

Standing in line at a cafeteria one day I overheard a colleague who habitually kept everyone annoyed at him remark: "Not many people around here like me, but *everyone* knows who I am." It was a sad comment, but he made it smiling and with a certain gallows pride. He was surviving on negative strokes. He was not being ignored. I haven't seen him in over ten years, and I never knew him well, but my prediction is that he is still annoying people and smiling wistfully.

If you think about your own circle of colleagues, you can probably identify some who are always getting positive strokes and enjoying others' company; some who habitually get negative strokes by keeping themselves and others on edge; and others who, no matter how impressive their performance, are never satisfied with themselves because they never quite meet all their own conditions (or others never quite meet all their conditions). These people probably don't realize what they are doing, but you can learn a lot by observing how they go about getting their strokes and noticing how you go about getting yours. This is another dimension of Process.

Topdogs and underdogs

Strokes are basic motivators on and off the job. I can't really "make" other people do or feel something (they can choose not to respond), but I can "invite" someone to do or feel something by giving or with-holding strokes.

On-the-job strokes can be used by both the *Topdog* (boss) and the *Underdog* (employee) to invite others to respond in given ways.

The Topdog's power to use strokes is more obvious (raises, repri-mands, and important assignments given or withheld).

The Underdog's use of strokes is more subtle but just as power-ful. The subordinate who sulks or withholds strokes (silent treatment) from the boss can use this manipulative technique very effectively *if* the boss chooses to fall for it.

You can't please everybody

Once we become aware of our unconscious patterns for getting strokes, and our legitimate need for strokes, we can consciously improve our approach. We can be more selective about who we choose to get strokes from and give ourselves permission not to please everybody.

Trying to please everybody is always a response to an archaic childhood demand because any aware adult knows it's impossible. People disagree and make contradictory demands. What pleases one displeases someone else. We have to make choices. By making choices we can eliminate situations where we waste energy unconsciously seeking superficial strokes from people (or from archaic phantoms in our heads) that we don't really need to please.

This sorting out can be extremely time-conserving. Answering the questions in the following exercise can help you begin to identify the phantoms you may be responding to and plan for a more productive use of your time.

Deciding who to please (an exercise)

- Think about what you do to get positive strokes on the job. Con-sider the things that habitually take up most of your time. Which are succeeding and which are failing in terms of bringing you rich and rewarding positive strokes?

- Where are the strokes coming from? Are they coming from some current and important other person (a superior or respected colleague), from yourself, or from some voice from the past inside your head?

- If the activity is not bringing satisfying strokes or is a response to some no longer relevant voice from the past at the expense of more important current needs, what can you do to eliminate it?

- What kinds of positive strokes are you not getting now, but would like to get? Are they more important to you than some less satisfying strokes you are now getting? Can you make trade-offs? What is the first action step in your contract with yourself to do this?

- Think about what negative strokes you are now getting. What is there in the situation that is inviting these? What is it you are doing (or not doing) that is helping maintain the situation? Who are the negative strokes coming from? Are they from some relevant person who really has influence in your life today?

- Are you replaying any negative strokes from the past? Are you giving yourself negative strokes for not meeting some archaic demands (e.g., "Be strong and don't have feelings or emotions. Men are not supposed to have feelings.") that were never real, or at least make no sense today? What can you do to eliminate these negative strokes? What would the first action step be?

- Now think about what conditional strokes you are receiving today. Most organizations are full of conditions, some real and many that can safely be ignored. Write down a list of the major conditions to which you currently respond. Study them. Sort them out, critical and not really critical. Make a personal reevaluation of which are reasonable and which are unreasonable, which necessary and which unnecessary. Forget for a moment what the organization or your boss thinks. What do you think?

- What can you do to eliminate some of the unreasonable or unnecessary conditions? Even if they are currently necessary, do you like them? Might you have outgrown some of them? Is it someone else's turn while you move on to other things that represent growth for you? What can you do to start the ball rolling on that?

Autonomy begins with questioning the conditions

Autonomy begins with questioning the conditions. Whose conditions are they? Do I want to respond? Do I have to respond? How can I find a practical way to quit responding when I don't like the conditions?

Evolving stages on the road to autonomy

If personal autonomy is a desirable attribute in the pursuit of career satisfaction, what precisely is autonomy? How can we recognize it in others and develop it in ourselves?

When there is confusion over what autonomy means—and this is frequently the case—there is often disagreement over whether or not it's really a desirable trait for individuals to display in organizations. Some see autonomy for individuals as a threat to organizations and fear its pursuit will keep an individual and an organization forever in conflict. This view comes from confusing true autonomy with a brand of selfishness and indifference to others' needs that often masquerades as autonomy.

Most of the confusion and disagreement are resolved when the term autonomy is clearly defined. Properly understood and exercised, autonomy is a great asset for any individual who seeks significant contribution and reward in an organizational setting. Also, autonomous employees, managed properly, are major assets to any organization.

The above became very clear to me several years ago when I heard Dr. Marvin Dunnette from the University of Minnesota address a group of manpower planners on the subject of assessing human performance. His definition of autonomy and the concepts he presented gave me a new set of criteria for observing the behavior of people in organizations. Calibrating what I observed against these criteria was most illuminating in terms of how people who get useful things done tend to behave differently from people who don't get things done.

From fear to self-actualization

Dr. Dunnette described autonomy as the end result in a series of growth stages in the ego development of individuals from passive fear to active and independent self-direction. He said the concept and measurement of ego development through these stages will probably become as fundamental to predicting an individual's success and achievement in our society as the concept and measurement of basic intelligence (I.Q.).[7]

Noticing which point on the ego development scale (shown in Table 6.1) represents the type of actions I devote most of my time

Table 6.1   Stages of ego development

Evolution up the scale to a mature autonomy ↑		
	Autonomous (self-actualizing)	Adult processing of current (non-archaic) data as an aid to growth
	Principle judgment	Behavior guided by principles
	Obedience	Rule-oriented
	Self-protective	Fear of punishment

to today and deciding where I want to be acting on the scale in the future can be an important first step toward becoming autonomous.

Ego development involves an individual's ability and approach in making moral judgments. Ego development unfolds through a series of stages from birth up into our forties.

Ego development evolves from avoidance of punishment to taking account of what's best for self and others in life. The scale of an individual's ego development is measurable and has been tested in experiments.

Not everyone continues evolving up this scale to autonomous behavior. Many freeze their own design and quit growing at one of the earlier stages.

Any large organization has people in all age groups operating at each of these ego development stages. Some are motivated by fear; some blindly and unquestioningly follow rules; some have unchanging principles that serve as roadmaps for everything they do; others are autonomously updating their roadmaps based on clear and ongoing perceptions of today's evolving realities.

In computer language, the self-actualizers continuously and flexibly plot and correct course based on "real-time" data coming in today, as opposed to compulsively following a canned or predetermined life program. They have clear, predetermined life programs and goals, but they continuously update them based on new data.

The autonomous people need not in any sense be unprincipled. They merely keep their minds open to new data and modify principles if new information shows an older decision needs updating. I may have grown up believing the principle that men should earn the living and women should always stay home with the children. That may have been true in some earlier environments, but it's a questionable premise today.

We can remain principled and still not freeze the design. All adult decisions are probability judgments based on information available when the decision is made. That is the best we humans can do.

If a principle originally accepted on the basis of an adult decision becomes a frozen attitude not open to new data and ongoing evaluation, that attitude can quickly rigidify into an archaic prejudice.

The autonomous self-actualizers keep their antennae out and their receivers on. They avoid reacting to archaic demands, or looking to any Big Daddys for direction in life. They consciously manage their time to accomplish the most possible of what they personally believe is important.

I once asked a consultant who worked in the corporate office selecting high-level general managers for GE what he looked for as the key ingredient for predicting success in general managers. He replied unhesitatingly and unequivocally, "enough self-confidence that they don't have to be right." By that he meant the individuals kept tuned in to today's realities, noticed mistakes, admitted them, corrected course without guilt or feelings of inadequacy, and got on with the job at hand. They were not defeated by errors and they didn't waste people's time denying or blotting out the realities of mistakes they had made. That's a form of autonomous self-actualizing that is very critical to anyone's growth as a person.

The self-actualizers have learned to monitor and control the many conflicting voices, past and present, in their heads. They know when they are role playing and when they aren't. They decide what demands in the environment they will and will not respond to. They keep their many roles consciously integrated to maintain a clear and whole self, with specific demands of its own. They know who they are. They work effectively at getting positive strokes in dimensions that are relevant to their personal value systems.

Learning autonomy

Very few people are autonomous self-actualizers. Those who are have a giant advantage over those who aren't both in finding self-fulfillment and in contributing to the rest of the world.

But how do we become autonomous? How do we break out of old nonproductive patterns and move up the scale of ego development? Why do some stop growing at lower stages than others?

Fortunately, identifying the roadblocks, overcoming them, and moving up the scale is learnable behavior.

As I recall, Dr. Dunnette didn't mention Transactional Analysis, but the theories of Eric Berne are very compatible with what Dunnette said.

Berne's discoveries give us valuable insights into how our personalities are structured and how this structure influences our self-generated freedom to behave autonomously.

Personality
structure   7

Recordings from the past

In identifying the major components of our personality structure, Berne picked up valuable insights from the experiments of Dr. Wilder Penfield, a Canadian neurosurgeon. Penfield had applied weak electrical stimulations to the bared temporal cortex of patients' brains when performing surgery on epileptics. The patients, under local anesthesia, were fully conscious and able to talk. The stimulations produced interesting results.

The patients were able not only to recall, but in effect to relive events that had happened in their past, some of which they couldn't even remember before the operation. In this "reliving," they experienced the same spontaneous, involuntary feelings of the original events. As Penfield explains it:

> The subject feels again the emotion which the situation originally produced in him, and he is aware of the same interpretations, true or false, which he himself gave to the experience in the first place. Thus evoked, recollection is not the exact photographic or phonographic reproduction of past scenes and events. It is a reproduction of what the patient saw, heard, and felt and understood.[8]

The memories forced into an individual's consciousness by the electrical stimulations seemed to be a present experience, and,

> Only when it is over may he recognize it as a vivid memory of the past.[9]

In commenting on Penfield's findings, Tom Harris, a psychiatrist who was one of the pioneers in the application of Berne's T.A. concepts in psychiatry, says:

> Perhaps the most significant discovery was that not only past events are recorded in detail, but also the feelings that were associated with these events.[10]

> Recollections are evoked by the stimuli of day-to-day experience in much the same way that they were evoked artificially by Penfield's probe. In either case the evoked recollection can be more accurately described as a *reliving*, than a recalling. . . . Following the experience a person may then consciously *remember* he was there. The sequence in involuntary recollections is: (1) *reliving* (spontaneous, involuntary feeling) and (2) *remembering* (conscious, voluntary thinking about the past event thus relived).[11]

Harris then explains that: "Much of what we *relive* we *cannot remember*."[12] In other words, often the involuntary recollection stops at the first (feeling) step. A stimulus in today's environment may cause me to relive involuntarily, and with high fidelity, a feeling or set of feelings associated with a past event; but I may not remember the event that originally caused these feelings.

The individual who writes overly detailed and perfect reports may not remember his or her fourth-grade teacher, but any current stimulus of having to write a report unconsciously arouses a reliving of the same fears of inadequacy, punishment, and rejection experienced when the intimidating teacher rejected an imperfect report. In responding to this now archaic fear from the past, the person's behavior moves down the scale from aware autonomy to unconscious fear of punishment. These involuntary replays of past feelings are influencing how he or she behaves today, counterproductively. The person works to please an old teacher when, in fact, today's report is for a current boss who much prefers conciseness.

If clearly articulating my point of view in disagreements with my parents brought on negative reactions that led to frightening feelings of rejection as a child, I may experience the same feelings and fears of rejection when stimulated by a need to articulate my observations on a controversial subject in a business meeting today. I may fearfully and repeatedly keep my mouth shut when, in fact, not contributing my observations may be the very thing that will lead to my being rejected, passed over, or denied opportunities for meaningful challenges today.

While archaic fears and feelings can be debilitating, they don't have to be. With the proper awareness and techniques, I can turn the tables and use them to my advantage. They can become windows I peer through for an increased awareness of myself, and clues to ways I can become more autonomous.

The following trackdown exercise shows one way disturbing feelings can be used as clues to how we can behave more productively in the future. I use this approach often, and I recommend it to you.

Trackdown (an exercise)[13]

When something is not going well and the situation is becoming repetitive (e.g., being afraid to speak up in business meetings), don't deny the situation or suppress the disturbing feelings associated with it. It's more productive to use these disturbing feelings as springboards for some insight-developing problem solving as follows:

1. *Experience the feelings*—Get in touch with exactly how you feel. Pinpoint and define the precise disturbing sensations. Allow yourself to experience them as fully as possible.

2. *Review the situation*—Look at what present reality or event triggered the disturbance.

3. *Evaluate relevance*—Ask yourself if the current situation is really sufficient reason in itself for the disturbing feelings (particularly for the intensity of the feelings). Is your reaction appropriate to what is happening today or is there some overreaction on your part?

4. *Trackdown*—When have you felt similar feelings in the past? What is the pattern of events that repeatedly triggers feelings of this type? When was the first time you can consciously remember feeling like this? What was the event? (You probably won't be able to recall the absolute first time, but it's helpful to at least specify the first time you *remember the feelings*.)

5. *Recognition*—What is it you bring to situations like this? What is it you tend to do, think, assume (or not do) that contributes to your feeling and reacting like this? If the feelings are repetitive

and you experience them in different situations with different people, one common thread to these experiences is you. You should at least think about what you are contributing.

6. *Separation*—Separate the "then" and the "now." Separate past events that triggered these feelings from today. Might what you are doing and feeling have been appropriate in some of those past situations, but not in today's realities? If so, how can you help yourself behave and feel more positively today?

7. *Redesign*—In similar future situations how can you behave more productively for you? What positive action steps can you take in what sequence (or what negative action steps can you avoid) to be more effective and make yourself feel better in similar future situations?

Identifying and reassessing the voices

It may be that even though my boss is polite, I sense in his or her body language and lack of specific praise a displeasure with my reports. The harder I work to perfect them the cooler my boss becomes. I should make a contract with myself to find an opportunity to ask for the boss' reaction to my reports: "I sense that somehow these are not exactly what you are looking for . . . I'd find it helpful if we could review them together and see how they might be improved to better meet your needs."

It would be even more helpful if I could remember my fourth-grade teacher and reassess his or her impact on my style. Berne's concept of basic ego states provides a simple, nonthreatening, and easily understood way to identify and reassess the voices (present and archaic) in my head. The ego states represent Berne's classification of our internal tape recordings into their most significant categories.

We'll look at the ego states next.

Three parts

Berne tells us that:

It is most fruitful to think of the human personality as being divided into three parts, or even better to realize that each individ-

ual is three different persons, all pulling in different directions . . .
so that it is a wonder anything ever gets done.*

Because the recordings discovered by Penfield have an effect on how
I behave today, I can do a more effective job of defining my most
important values and generating strategies to achieve them if I identify these recordings and sort them out.

In sorting them—and in helping hundreds of clients sort them—
Berne and his associates found that the tapes in each of us represent
three basic ego states.

Berne defines ego states as: "coherent systems of thought and
feelings manifested by corresponding patterns of behavior."[14]

He identifies the three ego states each individual exhibits as follows:

(1) Those derived from parental figures, colloquially called the
    Parent.[15]

(2) The ego state in which he appraises his environment objec-
    tively, and calculates its possibilities and probabilities on the
    basis of past experience, is called the *Adult* ego state. . . . The
    Adult functions like a computer.[16]

(3) Each person carries within a little boy or little girl, who feels,
    thinks, acts, talks and responds just the way he or she did
    when he or she was a child of a certain age. This ego state is
    called the Child.[17]

Berne makes an interesting observation on the Child.

It is important for the individual to understand his Child, not
only because it is going to be with him all his life, but because it
is the most valuable part of his personality.[18]

The positive parts of my Child ego state frequently and need-
lessly get discounted or lost in my work life; often at significant detri-
ment to my productivity, creativity, and real achievement.

I am operating in one of my ego states during every waking moment. I can switch rapidly back and forth among my ego states in
seconds, but I am always in one of them.

---

* From Eric Berne, *Sex in Human Loving*, p. 81. Copyright © 1970 by
the City National Bank of Beverly Hills, California. Reprinted by permission of Simon & Schuster, Inc.

Each of my ego states is important to me. I need all three to operate as a complete human being. The key to operating effectively and autonomously is to become aware of my ego states—learn to know which I'm in at a given time—and develop the ability to consciously switch to the ego state that will serve me most effectively in a specific situation.

Berne diagrams each individual's ego states with three circles as shown below.[19]

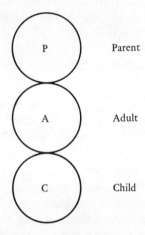

In T.A. the ego states are capitalized (*Parent*, *Adult*, and *Child*), to distinguish them from actual other people—parents, adults, and children. From here on, whenever we capitalize Parent, Adult, and Child, we'll be referring to the internal ego states inside my head, not to other actual people.

Each ego state has it's own unique set of characteristics. Let's look at each separately, beginning with the Parent. (Unless otherwise indicated, the quotations in these next sections on ego states will be directly from Eric Berne.)

The Parent

It should be noted that the Parent is exhibited in two forms, direct and indirect; as an active ego state, and as an influence. When it is directly active, the person responds as his own father (or mother) actually responded ("Do as I do"). When it is an indirect influence, he responds the way they wanted him to respond ("Don't do as I do, do as I say"). In the first case he becomes one of them; in the second, he adapts himself to their requirements.[20]

My Parent ego state is judgmental, all knowing, never in doubt. It consists of attitudes and behaviors I have recorded in uncensored fashion from external others such as my real parents, teachers, influential peers, or parent substitutes. The key to Parent ego state attitudes, beliefs, and behaviors is that they are untested. I have swallowed them whole from external sources without subjecting them to the critical analysis and data testing functions of my own intellect. I have not questioned, critiqued, analyzed, and verified their reality or appropriateness. Most of the data recorded in my Parent ego state was assimilated during my first five years and, as Tom Harris explains:

> The data in the Parent was taken in and recorded "straight" without editing. The situation of the little child, his dependency, and his inability to construct meanings with words made it impossible for him to modify, correct or explain.[21]

My Parent ego state speaks in absolutes and often in platitudes. In this ego state I use words such as should, ought, and always. I leave no room for questioning or new data.

My Parent helps me serve effectively as the parent of my own children, and it saves me a lot of time in the day-to-day process of living. It makes many useful responses automatic (e.g., maintaining personal cleanliness or not leaving loaded guns around children).

This frees my Adult computer from many trivial and repetitive decisions.

On the other hand, automatically believing that "men should not express their feelings" or that "only people of your own religion and race should be trusted" is archaic and not useful in my life today.

There are two parts to my Parent ego state: my *Controlling Parent* (CP) and my *Nurturing Parent* (NP).[22] Figure 7.1 illustrates traits of the Parent ego state.

My *Controlling Parent* ego state is telling, demanding, and critical of what it sees as mistakes (mine or others). It gives me and others the "do's and don't's," the stone tablets—but it doesn't bother to explain them.

Sometimes this is appropriate. Very young children may not be able to comprehend the reason for not playing with sharp knives or in

Fig. 7.1   Parent ego state (Controlling and Nurturing)

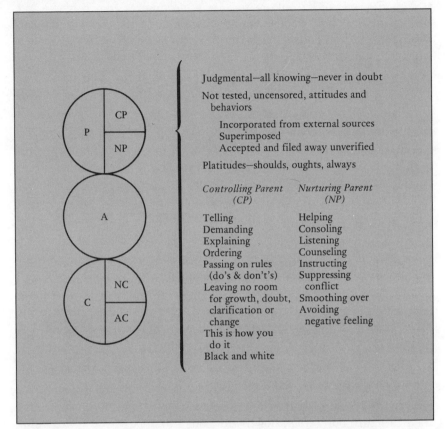

Judgmental—all knowing—never in doubt

Not tested, uncensored, attitudes and
   behaviors

   Incorporated from external sources
   Superimposed
   Accepted and filed away unverified

Platitudes—shoulds, oughts, always

Controlling Parent (CP)	*Nurturing Parent* (NP)
Telling	Helping
Demanding	Consoling
Explaining	Listening
Ordering	Counseling
Passing on rules (do's & don't's)	Instructing
Leaving no room for growth, doubt, clarification or change	Suppressing conflict
	Smoothing over
	Avoiding negative feeling
This is how you do it	
Black and white	

the street. They have to be told firmly. Commanders in battle don't
have time to explain all their orders. They expect unquestioning obe-
dience.

On the other hand, if my manager always gives orders from his
or her Controlling Parent without explaining the rationale (even when
there's time and I'm asking) that is not appropriate. I'm not learning
or growing and this does not utilize my intellect. Not being asked to
think, to use my intellect and make some of the important work decisions myself, is stifling and boring. If I want to continue growing,
and I can't break through this type of impasse with a manager who
spends too much time in his or her Controlling Parent, I'll be smart
to develop another job option and find a new manager.

If I am a manager myself, and I insist on staying in my Controlling Parent and thinking for my subordinates like this, I'll get tired a lot. I'll limit my growth as a manager to the size group I can think for. I'll also end up with some pretty weak subordinates, which will force me to work harder and get even more tired.

My *Nurturing Parent*, on the other hand, wants to take care of the Child in me and in others. My Nurturing Parent is helping, consoling—watching that my feelings don't get hurt. Positive strokes from my own or another's Nurturing Parent can be helpful at the right time. A child with a cut knee appreciates a Nurturing Parent's consolations. A boss who's just lost a big order may appreciate sympathetic listening from a secretary's Nurturing Parent.

My Nurturing Parent can also overdo it, however. Sheltering behavior may be an attempt to deprive me or someone else (a friend, child, spouse, or subordinate) of the growth experience that our meeting a difficult situation might bring. This is not helpful; it discounts my abilities and inhibits my growth.

Nurturing Parent superiors can smother my autonomy with love and concern (if I let them). This can be even more difficult to cope with than a Controlling Parent boss. Confronting differences with a boss whose Nurturing Parent behavior demonstrates clear concern for my welfare can involve feelings of guilt or ungratefulness (again, if I let it).

Identifying Parent influences (an exercise)

We can all operate much more autonomously if we take time now and then to figure out (track down) how our Parent ego states are influencing our career planning and make some conscious decisions about whether the results of this influence are what we really want. As practice in doing this I suggest you take a few minutes now and spontaneously complete each of the statements in the following exercise. Don't think about what the proper answers *should* be. No one but you will know what you say. Let the answers flow out in uncensored fashion. What are the first things that pop into your mind?

- A frequent way in which I express my Controlling Parent on the job is _____.

- A frequent way in which I express my Nurturing Parent on the job is _____.

- In telling me what my career should be, my natural parents (i.e., real mother and father) have always said _____.

- To date, my mentor's (most influential manager's) career advice to me has been that I should (speculate what he or she would say if no actual career discussion ever took place) _____.

- A frequent way in which my current manager expresses his or her Controlling Parent in giving me career advice is _____.

- A frequent way in which my current manager expresses his or her Nurturing Parent in giving me career advice is _____.

- Are there some archaic shoulds that are keeping you from confronting critical Process issues on the job (e.g., never disagree with the boss, always keep a low profile, keep personalities out of things)? What are they? List them.

- Where are you feeling anxiety in a repetitive situation? Are there any unreal shoulds or should nots in your head that are keeping you at an impasse and preventing you from developing solutions? Identify them and write them down.

- Are you doing anything you don't want to do because a real-world parent or manager wants it and you "shouldn't hurt people's feelings"? If they are loving parents or well-wishing managers, is that what they really want for you? Can you find a way to ASK? Are you ASSUMING incorrectly? Write down your assumptions and decide how you can test them.

Review your answers to the above questions. Look for trends and patterns, productive and nonproductive. Develop some action plans for eliminating the archaic and nonproductive influences so you can move on to more beneficial uses of your time.

Only I can live my life

Parents—the ones inside my head, my real ones, and my organizational supervisors—are OK in the right time and place. However, when Parent ego state *shoulds* (my own or other people's) become blocks or substitutes for my own aware thinking and autonomy, I'd better move into one of my other ego states for my planning, decision making, and fun. I can go right on loving my real parents and respecting my supervisors, but only I can live my life.

Let's look next at my Child ego state.

The Child

Berne said that: "In the Child reside intuition, creativity and spontaneous drive and enjoyment."[23]

If I make it possible, my Child can have fun on and off the job. Feeling good—feeling excited, joyous, adventurous, and creative—is fun. My Child is the ego state that feels. My Child ego state also contains the recordings of every feeling I've ever felt. As we mentioned earlier, when some external stimulus in today's environment causes me involuntarily to *relive* some event from my past, it is my Child's feelings that I relive, sometimes without recalling the event that originally produced them. My internal Child is the center of my emotions and my creativity.

Like my Parent, my Child ego state has two parts: my *Natural Child* (NC) and my *Adapted Child* (AC).[24] Figure 7.2 illustrates traits of the Child ego state.

My *Natural Child* contains my natural impulses. In this ego state I am self-centered and unfettered. I want what I want when I want it. I am joyous, creative, spontaneous, unguarded, and authentic. I am also authentically confronting, and I resist being constrained.

My *Adapted Child* is quite different. This ego state came into being sometime early in life when I began to notice that I was very small and dependent on all those giants called grown-ups for my physical survival. At that point, I accepted constraints and began to behave not as I wanted but as I perceived these big people expected me to behave. I began trying to please others at the expense of my own desires in the interests of safety and survival. Even today, when I move into my Adapted Child ego state I still see survival as pleasing all the big Parents in the world. I feel inferior, usually quite erroneously. I don't notice that all those other people also have Adapted Child ego states, and they are equally afraid of my big Parent. Even if I'm 30 and 6 ft. 4 in. tall, my Adapted Child ego state is still a helpless little 3- to 5-year-old—small, dependent, frightened, feeling inferior, and striving to please all those big people who, it believes, still control its fate. If I'm 30, of course, these feelings of smallness and inadequacy are hopelessly out of date. My Adapted Child doesn't

Fig. 7.2 Child ego state (Natural and Adapted)

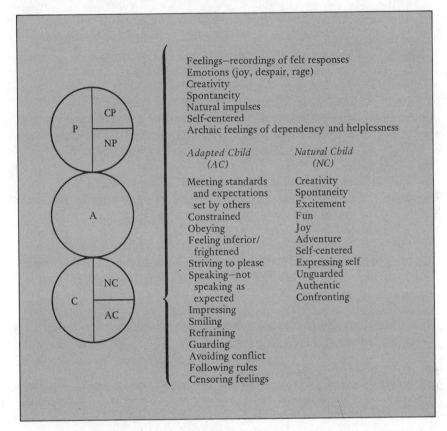

Feelings—recordings of felt responses
Emotions (joy, despair, rage)
Creativity
Spontaneity
Natural impulses
Self-centered
Archaic feelings of dependency and helplessness

Adapted Child *(AC)*	*Natural Child* *(NC)*

Meeting standards
  and expectations
  set by others
	Creativity

	Spontaneity
	Excitement
Constrained	Fun
Obeying	Joy
Feeling inferior/ frightened	Adventure
	Self-centered
Striving to please	Expressing self

Speaking—not
  speaking as
  expected
	Unguarded

	Authentic
	Confronting
Impressing	
Smiling	
Refraining	
Guarding	
Avoiding conflict	
Following rules	
Censoring feelings	

know that, however. I don't know that when I move into this ego state and give my Adapted Child executive (controlling) power.

Even if I'm already president of the company, my Adapted Child probably gets executive power inside me a great deal of the time.

On the job my Adapted Child ego state sees my manager and all authority figures as big Parents I must please. In this ego state I smile a lot so people know I like them. I strive to impress. I am guarded. I follow the rules. I censor my feelings and express only those I feel will be acceptable.

I speak or don't speak according to my Adapted Child's impression (often wrong) of what is expected. My Adapted Child checks things out a lot with my internal Parent. This internal dialogue some-times distracts me to the point where I don't have time to notice what's really happening in the here and now. That does not help my actual survival, but my Adapted Child doesn't notice that either. My Adapted Child lives in a very outdated and unreal world.

If I work in a large organization, my Adapted Child probably gets significantly more air time than my Natural Child on the job. Even in private moments, my Natural Child ego state may get little oppor-tunity to communicate its needs. My Natural Child gets preempted by the ongoing internal dialogue between my critical Controlling Par-ent and my insecure Adapted Child—by my preoccupation with "what's expected."

My Natural Child may be much more in tune with today's real-ities than my past-oriented Adapted Child. In that sense, my Natural Child can be much more pragmatic about what it takes to achieve both survival and satisfaction.

The *biggest roadblock to my success* and on-the-job self-fulfill-ment is not my Natural, but rather my Adapted Child. My Adapted Child doesn't want to confront conflict in situations when dealing appropriately with conflict is what I need most to get ahead. My Adapted Child preempts my Natural Child's spontaneity and flexibil-ity in situations where creativity and spontaneity are precisely what's needed for success.

Identifying Child influences (an exercise)

If we are to plan autonomously for our own job satisfaction today and in the future, we need to identify (track down) how both our Parent and Child ego states are influencing what we do.

You, the reader, can begin to analyze how your Child ego state influences your on-the-job behavior and career planning by taking a few moments to complete the statements in the following exercise. Again, don't think about what the proper answer *should* be. What are the first things that rush to your mind?

- A frequent way in which I express my Natural Child on the job is _____.

- A frequent way in which I express my Adapted Child on the job is _____.

- Ways my Natural Child has influenced my career planning to date are _____.

- Ways my Adapted Child has influenced my career planning to date are _____ .

- In future jobs my Natural Child wants more _____ .

- In future jobs my Natural Child wants less _____ .

- In my future career progression the main barriers to getting what my Natural Child wants more or less of will be _____ .

What's needed is clear thinking

In the Process of defining and getting what I want out of my work, what's needed is clear thinking. Neither my Parent nor my Adapted Child ego states are thinkers in today's here and now. Both are archaic and locked in the past. My Natural Child notices but is not a very systematic thinker.

How do I perceive today's reality and think effectively in real time (i.e., in the here and now)?

That's the function of my Adult ego state.

The Adult

The Adult ego state is my clear-headed, real-time, reality-oriented data processor and problem solver. Berne says the Adult:

> ... represents the voice of reason. It works like a computer, taking in information from the outside world, and deciding on the basis of reasonable probabilities what course of action to take and when to take it.*

> The Adult tells you when and how fast to cross the street, whether to raise or fold on a two pair, when to take the cake out of the oven, and how to focus a telescope. In crossing the street, for example, it works like a very accurate and very complicated computer, estimating the speeds of all the cars for blocks on each side, and then picking the earliest possible moment for starting across without being killed, or rather without having to lose your dignity by running.†

---

* From Eric Berne, *Sex in Human Loving*, p. 82. Copyright © 1970 by the City National Bank of Beverly Hills, California. Reprinted by permission of Simon & Schuster, Inc.
† Ibid., p. 83.

My Adult ego state has no emotions. In my Adult ego state my vision is unclouded. I look realistically and objectively at today's facts and make decisions. I compute the probabilities of what is right for me. I ask questions. I collect data dispassionately. I make trade-offs. When I give it the executive power, my Adult ego state can assume total control. Eric Berne says that no one has a weak Adult.

Figure 7.3 illustrates the traits of my Adult ego state.

Once I accept the fact that I have a strong Adult and learn I can give my Adult the executive power over my behavior at will, my Adapted Child can relax a bit.

The specter of my Controlling Parent becomes less scary. My Adult can handle that too. My Adult can test all my Parent tapes,

Fig. 7.3   Adult ego state (No one has a weak one.)

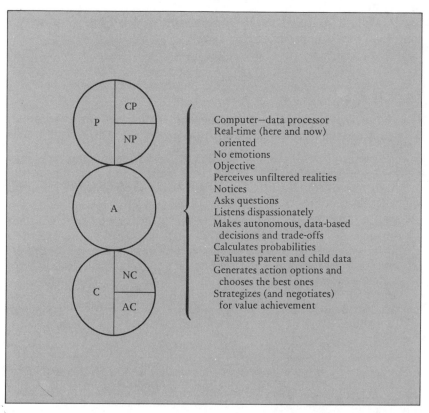

beliefs, attitudes, and behaviors against reality. My Adult can decide which make sense and which don't. This can free me to turn on my antennae and notice the real world of today.

It's important to know that in rejecting no longer appropriate Parent-type beliefs, I am not rejecting my actual parents. I'm testing my own internal habitual beliefs, attitudes, and behavior patterns. I'm not testing other people. I'm deciding which of my habitual beliefs and behavior patterns are still relevant today. Many of these came from people other than my parents. If the belief, attitude, or behavior checks out as still relevant, I can maintain it as part of my Adult data bank. If it's archaic (appropriate for a 5-year-old but not a 30-year-old), or if it never did make any sense now that I really look at it, I can free myself from its inhibiting influence.

Many of our religious beliefs, which started out as Parent injunctions when we memorized them in catechism class, can become very firm Adult convictions as we mature if we check them out in our Adult computer and decide consciously that the probabilities indicate they still make sense. Many are troubled by religion because they never apply their Adult ego state to the analysis of religious principles, but instead confine religion to an internal nonthinking Controlling Parent/ Adapted Child dialogue of fear that results in a compulsive, ritual submission or fearful rejection. Much of the joy we read about in the early Christians probably came from the Natural Child/Adult orientation their new convictions gave them.

My Adult can protect my Child. I can let my Natural Child ego state out to have more fun once I realize that my Adult can take over at any time to keep it out of trouble: another step toward recovery of self.

My Adult can be my own personal Santa Claus to get my Natural Child the most possible of what I really want.

With my Adult I can start now on that difficult but not boring job of tuning in on my dissatisfactions, noticing what it is I want that is missing, and strategizing for getting it.

My own version of self-fulfillment might be as president of a company, social worker, YMCA youth leader, charter-boat captain, craft- and candle-shop proprietor, lawyer, or teacher.

Success is what I want, whatever that is. Being president of a company when I'd rather be a teacher is not success. I've seen Ph.D. engineers go into real estate. One engineering Ph.D. went back to school for his M.D. One high-potential engineering manager really did open a candle shop. Many decide they want to become corporate executives, and then go about objectively investigating what that really means in terms of job content and what incumbents really did to get there.

Fig. 7.4 Ego states summary (Parent—Adult—Child)

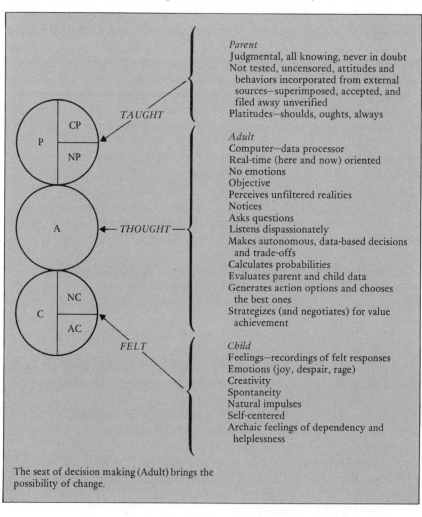

Parent
Judgmental, all knowing, never in doubt
Not tested, uncensored, attitudes and
    behaviors incorporated from external
    sources—superimposed, accepted, and
    filed away unverified
Platitudes—shoulds, oughts, always

Adult
Computer—data processor
Real-time (here and now) oriented
No emotions
Objective
Perceives unfiltered realities
Notices
Asks questions
Listens dispassionately
Makes autonomous, data-based decisions
    and trade-offs
Calculates probabilities
Evaluates parent and child data
Generates action options and chooses
    the best ones
Strategizes (and negotiates) for value
    achievement

Child
Feelings—recordings of felt responses
Emotions (joy, despair, rage)
Creativity
Spontaneity
Natural impulses
Self-centered
Archaic feelings of dependency and
    helplessness

The seat of decision making (Adult) brings the
possibility of change.

Autonomy takes practice

Even with a powerful Adult at my service, of course, life is not without problems. Autonomy is not an easy road to follow. It takes practice, perseverance, and tough decision making.

To begin with, I have to decide on my personal values. If some of these conflict, I have to make a choice of which are most important to me. I have to identify which I'm willing to give up if that's the price of breaking a no-action impasse and getting on with maximizing my own self-fulfillment.

I won't find Utopia, and there will still be compromises—particularly where financial obligations present real restraints. But at least the trade-offs can be conscious, and they can be my decisions (not the system's, Big Daddy's, or pure chance because I never took charge). That in itself is a rare and giant step forward.

Also, with autonomy, I tend to develop a new and potent awareness of what's really going on in the world around me; and learn how to get far more of my values realized than I ever suspect is possible when my Adapted Child is feeling passive, boxed in, and impotent.

Figure 7.4 summarizes the traits of the Parent, Adult, and Child ego states.

Berne notes that the Parent ego state contains images of an individual's actual parents as they were perceived by the individual as a helpless 3- to 5-year-old. That early and incomplete perception had many distortions about those big people. The internal Parent does not necessarily represent the reality of what the parents were like then (clearly not the total reality which the child was much too young to comprehend), and it certainly contains a different picture from the much broader, reality-oriented view I have when I look at my actual parents in my objective Adult ego state today.

Parents, mentors, and others 8

Many voices

By now it's clear I have many voices inside my head influencing my behavior. This isn't unusual. This is the human condition.

We've talked about Parent voices that come from real parents, teachers, bosses, and other figures of authority.

There is another uniquely influential Parent voice we should each evaluate with particular care. This may or may not involve someone who's had authority over us. This is the mentor.

I learned of the mentor phenomenon through studies conducted by Dr. Daniel J. Levinson of Yale University. He and his associates have studied the adult development of men over the age span of about 20 to 45.[25] They have identified specific stages of evolution in a man's life structure through the period of adulthood. The transitions from stage to stage often "occasion considerable turmoil, confusion, and struggle with the environment and within oneself."[26] Periods of crisis are predictable and even beneficial. Going through these crises can lead to significant creative gains.

One such time of crisis involves a man's separation from his mentors. Levinson and his associates tell us "the presence or absence of mentors is, we feel, an important component in a man's life course during the 20's and 30's."[27] They describe the mentor as follows:

> The mentor is ordinarily 8 to 15 years older than the mentee. He is enough older to represent greater wisdom, authority, and paternal qualities, but near enough in age or attitudes to be in some respects a peer or older brother rather than in the image of the

wise old man or distant father. He may be a teacher, boss, editor, or experienced co-worker. He takes the younger man under his wing, invites him into a new occupational world, shows him around, imparts his wisdom, cares, sponsors, criticizes, and bestows his blessing. The teaching and the sponsoring have their value, but the blessing is the crucial element.[28]

From apprentice to master

Throughout his twenties and well into his thirties, a man's life can be influenced strongly by his choice of mentors. During this period he is learning and establishing himself as a member of his trade or profession. The mentor (or mentors) serves in a role similar to that of master in the old master-apprentice system. During this period of developing his competence, a man spends much of his time learning from and attempting to impress relevant others who can influence his career progress (another period of asking what's expected).

To become a master himself, however, the apprentice must finally break from his master and set out on his own.

> The young man must in time reject this relationship, but this is largely because it has served its purpose. He is ready to take a further step in becoming his own man: to give up being a son in the little boy sense and a young man in the apprentice-disciple-mentee sense, and to move toward assuming more fully the functions of mentor, father, and peer in relation to other adults. This kind of developmental achievement is of the essence of adulthood . . .[29]

Sometime around the period between 35 to 39 the individual comes to realize he has been too subject to influence by those who have authority over him and too vulnerable to criticism. It is during this period that the relationship with the mentor changes. Levinson and his associates tell us:

> The final giving up of all mentors by those who have had them tends to occur in the middle or late 30's. One does not have mentors after 40. One may have friendships or significant working relationships after this, but the mentor relationship in its more developed form is rare, at least in our sample and in our life experience. It is given up as part of Becoming One's Own Man.[30]

Identifying mentor influences (an exercise)

In graduating from apprentice to master it helps to identify clearly in our own minds who our mentors are (or were); to analyze carefully what career and life value messages the mentors passed on to us; and then consciously to decide which of these messages we do and do not want to incorporate into our own adult career planning.

The following exercise can help begin this process.

- Think about this master/apprentice dynamic and identify your mentors. They may be current or past bosses, teachers, or respected senior colleagues in your field. Earlier we referred to your mentor as your most influential manager to date, but it could be someone else and you may have more than one.

- Think a moment and remember what key Parental messages your mentor gave you about what you should or should not do and be with respect to your career. Look at these messages (shoulds and oughts) very critically. Use your Adult to decide which you do and don't really agree with now. Are you letting any "musts" from current or former mentors influence your behavior in ways that are preventing your Natural Child from realizing other legitimate values that are more important to you? If so, how? What is your first self-initiated action step to improve things?

- If you no longer work for or with your mentor, are there still some Parent tapes in your head leading you in his or her direction rather than your own? What are they, and how will you minimize their influence in the future?

- If you haven't broken from your mentor, is the break overdue? Is it time to establish a direction of your own, perhaps quite different from your mentor's direction? How will you do this? What is your plan?

Stand on your mentor's shoulders

If you are young and your Adult tells you there is still much you can practically learn from your mentor, monitor constantly to be certain you are learning techniques on how to become your own person, not the mentor's mirror image. Look at how your mentor does things and keep yourself in the position of standing on his or her shoulders so you can extend your capabilities beyond your mentor's. If each generation doesn't do that, their mentors have failed.

The myth of omnipotence

Remember, no matter how helpful and considerate a mentor has been, this is your life not your mentor's. Although my mentor may be temporarily disenchanted if I decide to do things differently, he or she won't be destroyed by my independence. Despite my Adapted Child's unreal fears about this, I really don't have much control over what others feel and do. If I believe my actions can make mentors or anyone else feel good or bad, I suffer from the commonly believed "Myth of Omnipotence."

Apprentices break with masters every day. It may be temporarily traumatic, but the master (or mentor) usually finds a new apprentice quickly and life goes on.

It's traumatic when teenagers and young adults demonstrate their independence from their natural parents, but it's also a sign the parents have done their job. What natural parents really want a child still dependent on them when the child is thirty or forty?

From mentor to friend

After the trauma of separation, natural parents learn to brag about their children's independent successes and start to enjoy their grandchildren. After the break, most mentors learn to brag about the successful people they've trained and they find new apprentices. Objective parents and mentors learn to change their relationship with me from Parent/Child or mentor/apprentice to that of ongoing friend/equal. I can be independent and still enjoy their friendship.

If they chose not to allow this, that would be their decision and problem, not mine. That would be no reason for me to decommission my Adult and continue in my Adapted Child to please them. I needn't get angry. I can be understanding and friendly, but still firmly independent.

Useless competitions

Now let's look at another potential contaminating influence on your choice of values and career goals. This can be found in your own competitive instincts for being one-up on your friends, siblings, or peers. This is your relationship with your "others."

I learned the concept of my "other" from a pragmatic, down-to-earth compensation manager in industry. I went to work for him as an idealistic newcomer confident that statistical analysis could solve any problem. One day a dispute arose about a key employee's dissatisfaction with his raise. I presented volumes of data to prove the amount was correct in accordance with all my research and surveys. After listening he said: "I know that. So does he, but he's still unhappy. What raise did his 'other' get? It must have been more."

He then gave me his personal theory that every individual has some "other," usually someone close in age, against whom he or she is competing and measuring progress. The "other" may be a brother or sister, a college classmate, a neighbor, a friend in another organization, or a peer in the same organization. There may be more than one "other," and there is usually at least one in the individual's current organization.

If the individual is doing better than the "other," he or she is happy and satisfied, even if national surveys show both are paid low. If an individual does less well than he or she perceives the "other" is doing (and "others" do tend to exaggerate their progress), he or she is unhappy even if national trends show both are overpaid.

I can't prove this theory, but I believe it. I have a few "others," and I know how much it hurts when I think they are getting ahead of me. My Adult knows this is not rational, but it still hurts.

Races no one wants to be in

Hopefully, competition with my "others" is not making me trade off any of my top values just to keep up. Their values are probably and legitimately very different from mine. They may be paying a high price in some dimension (e.g., time with family) that's more important than money and prestige to me.

It's even possible they are trading off their own key values to stay ahead in a not-constructive competition with me (if I am their "other").

Maybe we are both sacrificing important values in a race neither of us even wants to be in. What a way to waste a life and lose a self.

If this is happening, where does it end? For me, it ends by getting into my Adult ego state and calling a halt. The others must determine how it will end for them. I can't be responsible for that. The following brief exercise can be helpful in eliminating unproductive results that stem from unnecessary competitions with others.

Avoiding useless competitions (an exercise)

- Who are your "others"? You probably have at least one. Identify them in your own mind.

- What price are you paying for the competition? What price is the "other" paying? Clearly articulate both in your own mind.

- Do you really want to race? What is the race doing to your Natural Child? Ask. If your Natural Child is hurting, put your Adult at your service and plan what has to be done differently in the future to avoid this useless competition.

Removing the pressures of conformity

Before I can realize authentic internal satisfaction in life (even if my outward accomplishments have been enormous), I must consciously define, follow, and be content with my personal values; and let my Parents, mentors, and others follow theirs.

Removing the pressures of conformity can remove enormous communications barriers. If we each can be our own person and be perceived as OK in this by our most important other people, our Natural Child ego states can enjoy each other more and our mutual strokes can become much more authentic, unconditional, and rewarding.

The best way to decide what my personal values really are is to listen to the drummer—my drummer. The drummer can tell me what values are uniquely important to me and in what rank order I can best make trade-offs when forced to make choices.

Listening to
the drummer   9

Where to find the drummer

In an earlier chapter I said the drummer is me—that core of inner reality that forms my own unique personality—that part of me that knows what I want independent of what anybody else expects of me.

Since that earlier chapter I've pointed out that there are many me's. I play many roles, react to many voices, and possess several ego states. Where in all that do I find the drummer?

The drummer resides in my creative, spontaneous Natural Child ego state, and I listen to the drummer most effectively from my Adult ego state. I find the drummer by engaging in an open two-way internal dialogue between my Natural Child and Adult ego states—a dialogue as free as possible of contaminations from my Parent and Adapted Child ego states. The best career plans are generated when I get a clear definition of what my Natural Child wants and put my Adult at my service to get as much of that as is possible and reasonable for me to have. This type of career plan will put me in work where I'll have the most fun and satisfaction. Also, since my energy will be flowing freely and naturally into what I do, this type of career plan will also put me in work where I'm likely to contribute and accomplish the most that is possible for me. (See Fig. 9.1.)

One of the most common roadblocks to productive career planning comes about when my Natural Child doesn't get enough air time; when the critical Natural Child/Adult dialogue is continually blotted out by the louder ongoing dialogues between my Adapted Child and my own and others' Controlling Parent ego states. (See Fig. 9.2.)

Fig. 9.1 A productive dialogue with the drummer

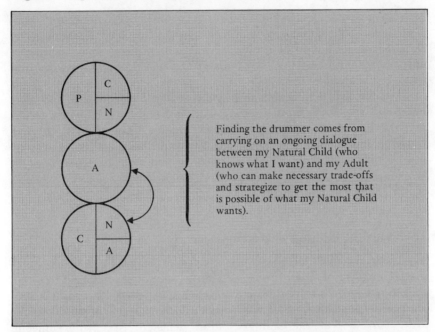

Finding the drummer comes from carrying on an ongoing dialogue between my Natural Child (who knows what I want) and my Adult (who can make necessary trade-offs and strategize to get the most that is possible of what my Natural Child wants).

Fig. 9.2 Contaminations that drown out the drummer

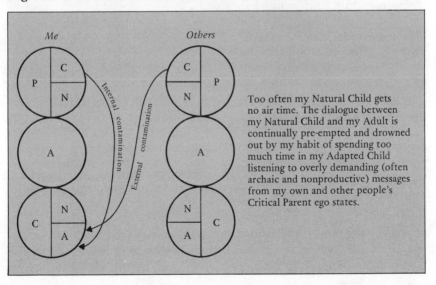

Too often my Natural Child gets no air time. The dialogue between my Natural Child and my Adult is continually pre-empted and drowned out by my habit of spending too much time in my Adapted Child listening to overly demanding (often archaic and nonproductive) messages from my own and other people's Critical Parent ego states.

My Natural Child wants everything

My Natural Child ego state wants everything, of course, and isn't concerned about the nonlogic of making contradictory demands. Why should it be? That's not its function. Its function is to be spontaneous, loving, and creative; to demand the world; to brainstorm and reach out with no restrictions.

My Natural Child ego state wants all the freedom of bachelorhood and the rewards of a loving wife and children. It wants to eat and drink everything good and never get fat. It wants to live in a small, intimate, southern academic town and have all the challenge, money, and status of a job that's only available in New York or Washington. It doesn't want to make decisions or choices. It wants Santa Claus (or Big Daddy) to let me have it all.

My Natural Child has preferences

My Natural Child does have preferences, however. Each of us wants some things more than others. Precisely what we want and in what rank order is distinctly different for each individual. Accepting someone else's—some organization's, "other's," supervisor's, or peer's—rank order isn't a Natural Child *or* Adult decision. Accepting someone else's rank order is laziness (unwillingness to think in my Adult), or Adaptive Child conforming behavior.

If I let my Child (Natural or Adaptive) wait for Santa Claus to give me everything, Santa won't come. Someone else (or blind chance) will make the trade-offs for me.

Both are really "nondecision" options, and both are dangerous for me. Letting chance or someone else make the trade-off will rob my Natural Child of many things I want most and substitute things I don't want nearly as badly.

Contradictions and impasses

My Natural Child needs help to recognize potential contradictions in things I want and to make Adult trade-off decisions that will at least preserve the things I want most.

If my Natural Child is at a value impasse (like the donkey starving between the two haystacks), there are usually signals—at least some vague feelings of uneasiness, boredom, irritability, and lack of potency or direction. The best way to break the impasse is to put my Adult in touch with my Natural Child's dilemma and make an action decision.

Action restores potency

Action restores potency. Action and decisions may temporarily raise anxiety, but they also relieve boredom. Anxiety, as we said earlier, usually accompanies positive change. I once heard a bored person who was using T.A. to break an impasse say, "I'm getting nervous. I must be doing something right."

After many years of career counseling, I've come to the conclusion that avoiding the value trade-off decisions—stepping aside and letting fate or the organization make them instead—is one of the *prime barriers to finding career satisfaction.*

If I don't make the decision myself, I set myself up for the emotional racket of being disappointed no matter what the decision is, particularly if the decision involves a life-value trade-off. It's a perfect corner. No matter what value is traded off, I can feel angry, put-upon, disappointed, cheated, and, most of all, impotent. I'm helpless at the whim of a bureaucratic system or a cruel fate.

This is nonsense, but organizations are full of grown men and women behaving and feeling just like this. Personnel workers spend hours listening to them, usually in confidence because they don't want their bosses to know how they feel.

Remember, no one has a weak Adult. That includes me. I can use my Adult and make my trade-offs. There will always be temporary setbacks—a lost contract or layoff in a location I want most. I may have to detour now and then, but over the long haul I can use my Adult to strategize and take action to get my Natural Child the most possible of my important values.

Deciding the drummer's values (an exercise)[31]

You can get some practice at what hopefully will become a lifelong and very articulate internal dialogue between your Natural Child and Adult ego states by completing the following exercise which is designed to help you identify and define your drummer's most important values.

Table 9.1 shows a sample of 15 key values people typically want to realize for themselves. If your Natural Child ego state is like mine, it wants them all. Unfortunately, I can't have them all. Some people will realize more of these than others, but no one will realize them all

Table 9.1   Sample life values*

(Recognizing potential contradictions and making cooperative Adult/ Natural Child trade-off decisions to break the impasses and renew forward movement)

- *Friendship*—To work with people I like and to be liked by them.
- *Location*—To be able to live where I want to live.
- *Enjoyment*—To enjoy my work, to have fun doing it.
- *Loyalty*—To be loyal to the company and to my boss and to have their loyalty in return.
- *Family*—To have time with my family.
- *Leadership*—To become an influential leader.
- *Achievement*—To accomplish important things, to be involved in significant undertakings.
- *Self-realization*—To do work that is personally challenging that will allow me to realize the full potential of my best talents.
- *Wealth*—To earn a great deal of money and be financially independent.
- *Expertness*—To become a known and respected authority in what I do.
- *Service*—To contribute to the satisfaction of others. To help people who need help.
- *Prestige*—To be seen as successful, to become well known, to obtain recognition and status in my chosen field.
- *Security*—To have a secure and stable position.
- *Power*—To have the authority to approve or disapprove proposed courses of action, to make assignments and control allocation of resources.
- *Independence*—To have freedom of thought and action, to be able to act in terms of my own time schedule and priorities.
- ....
- ....
- ....

---

* Developed by Kaye Matthews and Austin DeGroat of General Electric's Aircraft Engine Group.

because several are likely to contradict each other. This isn't because some Big Daddy is plotting mean things. This is simply because that's the way the world is. My Parent will criticize this situation and my Child won't like it—but my Adult can recognize and deal with this unpleasant reality pretty matter of factly. If I let it, my Adult ego state can dispassionately and without inappropriate, energy-wasting blaming, process the data, consult my Natural Child ego state about its desires, arrange a hierarchy, and plan to get the best and the most of what's possible.

In this exercise find out what your Natural Child really wants, whether or not it's practical.

Step 1
Before reading further, get some 3 x 5 cards or small pieces of paper. Write each of the fifteen values listed in Table 9.1 on a separate card. Don't necessarily limit yourself to the fifteen cards. If there are other important values in your life not on our list, write each of them down on a separate card. To start with, however, I suggest no more than twenty cards.

Step 2
Get in touch with your Natural Child and rank order these cards in order of their importance to you. Put the most important value (the one you'd be least willing to give up) on top and the least important on the bottom. Don't debate too much. Be spontaneous. Allow yourself no more than ten minutes for the initial ranking of all cards. When you finish your initial ranking, stop and review it.

Step 3
Assume your situation is such that you have to give up five of these values. Which would they be? Drop them out.

Remember this is your Natural Child sorting. Make certain your ranking represents your values. Forget what your parents, mentors, "others," peers, boss, or organization might suggest you value. For now, forget even the practicalities of earning a living. Pick your own personal, best of all values. Look on this as a candy store. Choose in the same self-serving way a five-year-old would choose there. Assume what's good for you is good for the world. This should give you some new perspectives on things.

Step 4

Look at the five cards you dropped. Who really dropped them? Which ego state? Was it really your Natural Child or were they dropped by your Controlling Parent, Nurturing Parent, or Adapted Child? How closely does your ranking resemble the things you identified earlier that your parents, boss, or mentors told you to be and do? Is what they (whoever "they" are) want really what you want? You don't, I hope, tell them what to be or want.

Think about that, and feel free to change your ranking. Who's looking?

Your Natural Child, of course, doesn't really want to drop any. That's why you need to keep your Adult and Natural Child in dialogue together. Your Adult will help you make certain you drop the values your Natural Child can most easily do without.

Step 5

Drop another card. If you started with fifteen cards, get down to nine.

If you were in one of our workshops, we'd have you working in groups of four comparing notes and discussing your reasons after each drop. This would be helping your Adult collect and process data from your Natural Child.

You'd be dropping different cards in different sequences than the others would be dropping. We'd be reinforcing the fact that this difference was OK. We are each different. If all in a group of four continue to drop similar cards in similar sequences, we check to see if some unconscious group norm isn't developing as a surrogate Parent and telling them what to do. You'll find this exercise more valuable if you get someone else to do it along with you and discuss the differences in the order you drop the cards.

Step 6

Drop another card. Now you're down to eight. Discuss the dropped cards if you are doing this with someone else. Tell them your reasons. Hear their reasons for what they dropped. Exchange data. Data processing helps keep your Adult in charge. By now your Adapted Child may be feeling scared and trying to take over. Your Adapted Child doesn't like the responsibility of making choices.

Don't feel obliged to drop your cards in reverse order to your original ranking. As you consider each time which card to drop, this process should surface new data. As your Adult gets more and more in touch with your Natural Child, your original ranking may change. It does for most people.

Step 7
Drop another card. Get down to seven. By now it's getting more difficult to decide. Discuss what you dropped or, if you're alone, think about the reasons. Let your Adult and Natural Child have a good gab fest.

Step 8
Drop another card, and get down to six. Discuss it or think about it by yourself again. Are there any new feelings or insights emerging?

Step 9
Drop another card. Stop at five. If you added cards, keep going one at a time until you get down to five final cards.

Step 10
Look at your final five cards. Rank order them. Think about why you kept these particular values. What do they mean to you? What's in them for your Natural Child? Change cards if this gives you new data or insights.

Are you achieving these five most important values for yourself now? Are you on a career path that will achieve them for you as you go along day by day? If so, how? If not, why not? What can you do to improve things? Don't wait for retirement to start living. You can start much sooner.

Step 11
Identify obstacles that are preventing you from achieving any of your five top values. Brainstorm this for a few minutes. Make a laundry list. Rank order the obstacles—most difficult to overcome first and least difficult last. You are acquiring more data for your Adult to use later.

Step 12
Write your five final values down on a piece of paper in rank order. Under these write your number 6 value, the one you dropped last. Go down the entire list and write your number 7, 8, 9, etc., values until

you have all 15 (or more if you added cards) listed in the final order you dropped them.

Look at your list. Any surprises? Think about your final ranking a while.

Adult contingency planning

After you've completed the above exercise, put your list aside but keep it. We'll look at it again later. This is Adult contingency planning—deciding in advance what you'll give up in what order if a conflict or impasse forces a decision.

An invitation to communications

The above is an interesting exercise (and an invitation to communications on important issues you probably don't often discuss together) to do with your spouse. Articulating your values to someone else forces you to organize your thoughts. This gives you new insights on the reasons behind your choices.

Avoiding Russian Roulette

These are some of the toughest decisions we have to make in life. No organization or Big Daddy can realistically make these trade-offs for us. When we leave these decisions to organizations, we leave our most personal choices in life to blind chance. It's a form of particularly destructive Russian Roulette.

Let's hope your Adult can get your Natural Child more than just the final five values. But let's not dream we can have them all, or get immobilized when the impasses arise. Obviously, my Adult can at least do better than blind chance.

We all have our share of impasses. What separates the autonomous from the bored is what, if anything, we decide to do about them.

My job—and the drummer's job—is not completed when I've simply identified my personal life-value priorities. I still have the task of selecting a career path that will allow me to realize my values.

References

Part 2

Chapter 6

1. From R. Spitz, "Hospitalism: Genesis of Psychiatric Conditions in Early Childhood," *Psychoanalytic Study of the Child*, 1945, 1:53–74.
2. From Eric Berne, *Games People Play* (New York: Grove Press, 1964), p. 15. Reprinted with permission.
3. Ibid., p. 14.
4. Ibid., p. 14.
5. Ibid., p. 15.
6. Ibid., p. 15.
7. Marvin D. Dunnette, Lecture on *Assessing and Describing Human Performance,* delivered at the General Electric Company's Management Development Institute, Crotonville, N.Y., 1971.

Chapter 7

8. From W. Penfield, "Memory Mechanisms," A.M.A. *Archives of Neurology and Psychiatry* 67 (1952): pp. 178–198, with discussion by L. S. Kubie, et al. Copyright 1952, American Medical Association.
9. Ibid.
10. From Thomas A. Harris, *I'm OK-You're OK* (New York: Harper & Row, 1967), p. 7. Reprinted with permission.
11. Ibid., p. 7.
12. Ibid., p. 7.
13. The *Trackdown* sequence presented is a slight modification of a procedure Helene Aronson outlined in one of her 1972 Philadelphia lectures.

14. From Eric Berne, *What Do You Say After You Say Hello?* (New York: Grove Press, 1972), p. 11. Reprinted with permission.
15. Ibid., p. 11.
16. Ibid., p. 12.
17. Ibid., p. 12.
18. Ibid., p. 12.
19. Ibid., p. 12.
20. From Eric Berne, *Games People Play* (New York: Grove Press, 1964), p. 26. Reprinted with permission.
21. From Thomas A. Harris, *I'm OK-You're OK* (New York: Harper & Row, 1967), p. 19. Reprinted with permission.
22. From Eric Berne, *What Do You Say After You Say Hello?* (New York: Grove Press, 1972), p. 13. Reprinted with permission.
23. From Eric Berne, *Games People Play* (New York: Grove Press, 1964), p. 27. Reprinted with permission.
24. From Eric Berne, *What Do You Say After You Say Hello?* (New York: Grove Press, 1972), p. 13. Reprinted with permission.

Chapter 8

25. Daniel J. Levinson, Charlotte M. Darrow, Edward B. Klein, Maria H. Levinson, Braxton McKee, "The Psychological Development of Men in Early Adulthood and the Mid-Life Transition," *Life History Research in Psychopathology*, Volume 3, edited by D. F. Ricks, A. Thomas, and M. Roff, University of Minnesota Press, 1974, pp. 243–257.
26. Ibid., p. 249.
27. Ibid., p. 251.
28. Ibid., p. 251.
29. Ibid., pp. 252–253.
30. Ibid., p. 252.

Chapter 9

31. The workshop game of sorting the *Sample Life Values* on cards for discussion in small groups was developed by Kaye Matthews and Austin DeGroat of General Electric's Aircraft Engine Group.

Selecting a career path

Part **3**

From tiring busyness to energy-generating growth in directions I choose to go.

Taking charge 10

Successful careers seldom happen by chance

Successful careers seldom happen by chance. With very few exceptions people who really get what they want in a career do so because they define clear objectives, develop plans and schedules for achieving their objectives, assume personal responsibility for implementing and following these plans, monitor their progress regularly, improve their plans when they aren't getting the desired results, and persevere in the face of frequent setbacks until their objectives are achieved. They do not wait for things to happen to them—they take charge. They do not spend all their time responding to unanticipated events not of their making. They find ways to anticipate future events and influence them in advance. They have learned how to escape a purely reactive mode of living and become more proactive.

From tiring busyness to energy-generating purpose

Proactive and reactive are two popular words in organization and behavioral science circles. What precisely do they mean?

Proactive is a conscious, deliberate, active taking charge and pre-planning of what I will do and accomplish. Reactive is a passive, unplanned, after-the-fact mode of living wherein I spend most of my time reacting to events after they have occurred.

Proactive is looking ahead and strategizing to avoid potential problems. It's deciding in advance how I will allocate my time for getting what I want. Reactive is wheel spinning. It's repetitive action devoted to resolving the same or very similar problems over and over again.

Reactive is firefighting (much of it in my Adapted Child) that keeps me so occupied I don't have time to think about what's causing the fires. Proactive is standing back and using my Adult to look for pattern, analyze the data, find the kid who's starting the fires, take away the matches, and move on to more meaningful uses of my time.

Reactive is busyness often accompanied by strong feelings of self-righteousness, martyrdom, self-sacrifice, and anger at less busy people who aren't "carrying their share of the load." Reactive is energy draining and tensely tiring, but not very productive or rewarding. Proactive brings the highest probability of accomplishment, self-satisfaction, and fun. Real accomplishment (i.e., meaningful to me) is energy generating and personally rewarding. Self-satisfaction (of my values) leads to a relaxing (not tense) tiredness followed by an eagerness to take on the next task.

In a management workshop dedicated to the proactive theme, I once heard Dr. Warren Schmidt, from the University of California at Los Angeles, lecture on proactive change. What he said helped me understand how some people manage to improve their mode of living from harried activity to satisfying progress.

Three time planes

Dr. Schmidt explained that there are three types of change in our lives, focused on three different time planes—the *past*, the *present*, and the *future*.[1]

When we speak of change in the *past* time plane, we refer to change that involves adjusting or adapting to events that have already occurred.

When we speak of *present* change, we mean initiating or influencing events that are happening now.

Change in the *future* time plane refers to anticipating and planning future events.

Figure 10.1 illustrates these different types of change.

How we allocate our time and efforts among these different time planes determines whether we are operating in a proactive or reactive mode.

If we spend most of our time reacting to events (not originated by us) that have already occurred, some (but not much) time initiating events in the present, and little or no time planning what we will do in the future—we are behaving *reactively*.

Fig. 10.1   Change has three time planes (From Warren H. Schmidt, *Lecture on Dealing with Youth's Changing Values,* delivered at the General Electric Company's Management Development Institute, Crotonville, N.Y., 1971. Used with permission.)

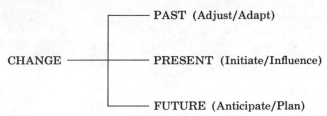

If we consciously manage our efforts so we can spend minimum time reacting to past events, devote more time to actively initiating and influencing what we do today, and make this possible by spending most of our time anticipating and planning future events to avoid nonproductive, repetitive wheel spinning—we are behaving *proactively*.

Figure 10.2 illustrates *reactive* versus *proactive* time allocation.

Clearly it's more rewarding and productive to behave proactively. Why then do some people spend the majority of their time in the wheel-spinning mode while others proactively set out to achieve their values and get it done?

Barriers

Some of the most predictable barriers to proactive identification and achievement of my personal values are:

- Nonproductive interventions of inhibiting and unverified Parent tapes.

- Not getting in touch with my Natural Child to find out what I really want (no goal or someone else's goal for me).

Fig. 10.2   Time allocation (From Warren H. Schmidt, *Lecture on Dealing with Youth's Changing Values,* delivered at the General Electric Company's Management Development Institute, Crotonville, N.Y., 1971. Used with permission.)

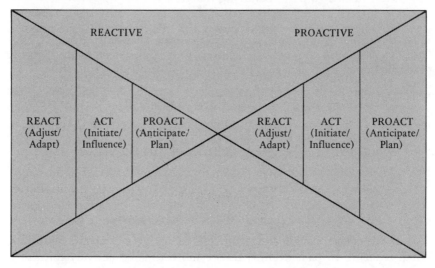

- Not using my Adult to plot a course, receive data, correct course based on identified (and admitted) mistakes, and make optimum trade-off decisions when I reach value impasses.

- Letting my Adapted Child stay in the executive power too much of the time—blotting out useful feedback on mistakes, trying to please everybody (but me), and avoiding necessary risks and issue confrontation with authority figures.

- Not developing a sufficient repertoire of persuasive human relations and communications techniques to get what I want (and enable me to effectively take risks and confront issues).

If I can eliminate most of these easily predictable barriers, I can free my Adult to plot the best possible course around unpredictable barriers such as natural disasters, illness, or economic fluctuations. Autonomy requires accepting responsibility for doing at least this, for me.

Response-ability

It's much easier to accept responsibility if you spell it differently. This was one of the most unforgettable lessons I learned in attending Helene Aronson's advanced T.A. training. She taught us to separate the word into two parts: response-ability.[2]

My Child (Natural *and* Adapted) backs off when I drop the hyphen and run this word together. Responsibility may connote a burden, something to bog me down and limit my freedoms.

Response-ability (i.e., my ability to respond and take action to guide my life) is the foundation for all my freedoms. My ability to respond to life's challenges with my own creative plan, with my self-developed options, and with my built-in Adult feedback and guidance system to maneuver around the barriers is autonomy.

A winner, faced with barriers, develops options to overcome them. Success is not a barrier-free life. Success and self-fulfillment come from the personal growth involved in overcoming barriers.

The first major barrier to be overcome on the road to achieving personal values at work is deciding what I want to do with the rest of my career. I need a roadmap for making that decision.

Deciding
what I
want to do 11

A roadmap for decision

Table 11.1 shows the roadmap we will follow in this section devoted to identifying (and reality testing) what I want to do. I start by systematically looking, in as unfiltered a fashion as possible, at history. What have been my peak satisfactions in life to date? What accomplishments of mine so far have been most meaningful to me (not to some supervisor, mentor, organization, or any other Parent)?

- *In Step 1*—I identify my 5–10 peak accomplishments in life to date (on or off the job).

- *In Step 2*—I use these accomplishments as clues to what type of things I most enjoy doing. On each peak accomplishment I identify what key muscles (intellectual, technical, interpersonal, physical, analytical) I was using. What specifically was I doing that felt so satisfying?

- *In Step 3*—I look for patterns in the data generated by steps 1 and 2. Using this data as a guideline (and considering also what new muscles I want to start exercising) I project myself 5–10 years into the future and decide what muscles I'd like to be exercising in an ideal work day or week then. I don't try at this point to identify specific jobs or titles. I simply decide generically how I ideally want to be spending all that time I'll be devoting to work.

The results of Step 3 along with my top five identified life values become my *Generic Job-Content Objectives*. These are then my criteria against which I can judge whether or not the actual content of potential future jobs is what I want. The work that will allow me to utilize the most possible of the muscles I like exercising best, and at the same time allow maximum possible realization of my personal values, will represent the best possibility.

I still haven't looked behind doors, however. I don't really know which of the potential career paths (in or out of my organization) actually has the content to meet my criteria.

Here I move into basic scientific experimental procedure. I form hypotheses, and then go out and collect data to prove or disprove my hypotheses.

- *In Step 4*—I form hypotheses. Based on the limited data available to me now, I speculate on what specific jobs will actually provide the content to satisfy my criteria 5–10 years out. I identify specific people who currently hold, or have successfully held, these specific jobs.

- *In Step 5*—I selectively look behind doors. I interview these people (using a specific format we'll provide later) to identify the actual job content (challenges, frustrations, muscles exercised, values achieved) of the jobs I identified. If the content doesn't meet my criteria (e.g., if the job requires 80 percent travel and I want no part of that), I cross that door off my list and move on. If the content meets enough of my criteria to represent a possibility, I continue the interview to determine how the incumbent got there and what the specific knowledge and experience requirements are in his or her eyes. I interview several different people holding those types of jobs I begin to zero in on as the strongest possibilities, and I compare their answers.

- *In Step 6*—I analyze all the data from my interviews and zero in on the specific career path I want most to follow from here on. (Several have used this for retirement planning).

- *In Step 7*—I identify potential next-step options to fill in gaps on required experience, training, and skills I need to qualify for the path I've selected.

- *In Step 8*—I develop specific strategies and options to make all this happen in a world where it takes a lot of clout and persuasion

Table 11.1   A roadmap for decision
(Option identification and development)

Past

	(Step 1) Peak Accomplishments	(Step 2) Muscles Exercised
	• _____	• _____
	• _____	• _____
	• _____	• _____
	• _____	• _____
	• _____	• _____

Present

(Step 3)
Generic Future Job-
Content Objectives
(Muscles I want to be exercising
5–10 years from now on the job)

	• _____	• _____
	• _____	• _____
Future Job- Content Criteria	• _____	• _____
	• _____	• _____

Top-ranked life values
career should allow me
to fulfill at minimum

• _____
• _____
• _____
• _____
• _____

Future

↓

(Step 4) Specific Future Career-Path Hypotheses
(What career path—which doors—will meet above criteria)

↓

Table 11.1   *Continued*

(Step 5) Reality Testing
(Structured interviews with incumbents and data collection
to verify which career paths do actually have the content to
satisfy my criteria—and what experience, training, skills
requirements are)

↓

(Step 6) Refined Specific Career-Path Choice
(Informed—data based—choice of which specific career path
I want to pursue from here on)

↓

(Step 7) Option Development
(Identify potential next-step options to fill in gaps on required experience, training, and skills)

↓

(Step 8) Option-Placement Strategies
(Develop strategy to enable movement into one of identified
next-step options and continue growth in direction *I* choose)

↓

Action—Ownership—Potency—Autonomy

to get what I want. (We'll be devoting later chapters to procedures for accomplishing this).

It isn't selfish

Identifying and creating action plans to get what I want in my career
is not selfishness. If you have a Parent tape that says strategizing to
get what you want is selfish, take a critical look at the reality of that
tape. People who find ways to do what they like to do contribute
more to society than they would forcing themselves, inefficiently and
with great waste of energy, to do something they don't like.

People who achieve personal values invite others (spouses, children, friends, and work associates) by example to do the same.

Pleasing your Natural Child on the job invites others to please
their Natural Child. This invites less friction, less negative competi-

tion, less fighting, even less warfare (little and big). It also invites significantly increased creativity and productivity.

Be unselfish. Allow yourself to strategize for finding work your Natural Child enjoys. If you allow yourself you'll allow others. That's friendly and it's helpful.

Our next few sections will involve specific exercises you can use to accomplish each step of the roadmap.

Spend some time on these exercises and do them; if not right now, then after you've completed this book and want to get down to the real work of planning the rest of your life proactively.

These exercises can be useful for people just entering the work force from school, but they are in no way limited to that age group. I've used them primarily with people who have from five to twenty years of organizational experience since school and, as we mentioned, several have found this approach particularly useful for planning their retirements.

Let's follow the roadmap in more detail now, one step at a time.

Recognizing past satisfactions (an exercise)

I said that "What do I want?" is a question many, perhaps most, in large organizations never realistically address and answer for themselves. We've learned to ask the self-alienating substitute question, "What's expected of me?" and searched in vain for someone to answer; or made the worse mistake of accepting answers from systems or other people who have no possible way of knowing what will be uniquely fulfilling for us.

Others can supply data, but when I get down to evaluating data and making personal decisions, I'm on my own. The only "theys" who can do that for me are my internal Adult and Natural Child ego states.

We've seen that my Natural Child ego state is creative but not well organized. How can my Adult get in touch with it and pin it down? I need a disciplined, systematic approach to get that done.

The first clue to where I want to go from here is to look at history. Where have I been so far? Which of my past accomplishments or achievements have been most satisfying to me? That's the starting point. Let's give it a try.

Looking back over your entire life, what have been your peak accomplishments to date? Think about this. Brainstorm and list as many as you can. Most people can list about five, or at most ten accomplishments that were honestly meaningful to them.

In listing these accomplishments carefully maintain the criterion of what meant the most to you personally (not to a parent, teacher, mentor, manager, organization, or anyone else). What accomplishments have given *you* the most personal satisfaction, whether or not anyone else shared your enthusiasm for them?

One clue will be how well these accomplishments satisfied your top-ranked life values. Another clue is how much your Natural Child enjoyed them.

If my Natural Child is involved and having fun, my energy and enthusiasm run high. I want to do what I'm doing.

When my Natural Child is not involved and I'm forcing myself to do something, my energy runs low. I feel the effort. It bogs me down. I look for excuses to avoid the activity.

Your most satisfying accomplishments may or may not have anything to do with your field of work. They may have been in school, in athletic or artistic activities, in social events, in community or local volunteer government work, in crafts, or part time hobbies.

Don't be modest. Give your Natural Child free rein when you make your list.

Table 11.2 shows a form you can use for this exercise.

Some examples of peak accomplishments are:

- Completed my degree.

- Wrote a play and participated in its production by a little theatre group.

- Helped reorganize the PTA at my children's school and developed a charter that gave the organization concrete goals to pursue.

- Coached a little league baseball team and watched the players' skill and self-confidence really develop.

- Designed a new computer-programming system that saved the company thousands of dollars.

- Succeeded in my first manager's job. Met the challenge.

- Presented a paper at a national meeting of my professional society.

Table 11.2   Recognizing past satisfactions (peak accomplishments)

List below between 5 and 10 of the most significant (to you) accomplishments of your life to date (on or off the job) based on the criterion of what was most meaningful to you (not necessarily to a manager, an organization, or anyone else). What achievements gave you the most personal satisfaction whether or not anyone else shared your enthusiasm for them? One clue will be how well they satisfied your life values.

● _____

   _____

   _____

● _____

   _____

   _____

   _____

● _____

   _____

   _____

   _____

● _____

   _____

   _____

   _____

● _____

   _____

   _____

   _____

● _____

   _____

   _____

- Played on a championship bowling team.

- Restored an old house—or boat.

- Restaffed and reorganized a poorly performing group to make it a recognized producer again.

- Made a state of the art breakthrough in my technology.

I could list pages of examples without repetition, but you can pick it up from here.

Again, be sure your list represents you. Look for intrusions of archaic Parent tapes from any external sources and factor them out.

After you complete your list, review it and boil it down to those top items that most represent your values. Rank order the accomplishments you choose according to which was the most meaningful to you, the next most meaningful, and so on down the list. This is your basic foundation for our next step.

Preferred skills (an exercise)

I use my peak accomplishments to date as starting points for what I want to do in the future.

I can't just repeat my past achievements. I can't graduate from college or succeed in my first manager's job again. I can, however, look at what muscles I enjoyed exercising in achieving these things and use this data to start identifying what muscles I want to exercise (i.e., what dimensions of challenge I want to take on) in future jobs.

Look at your top-ranked accomplishment. What was there about you that enabled you to do that? What were you actually *doing* in that accomplishment?

What muscles (intellectual, emotional, interpersonal, technical, analytical, physical) did you exercise in doing it? What were the key dimensions of this specific challenge that excited you and made it rewarding? This will be be important data for your Adult to compute in analyzing what you enjoy and do well. This will help you tune in on your key strengths.

Don't be modest about strengths. Career success is a function of strength management. This requires, at a minimum, identifying your strengths.

Let's look at an example. Suppose your top accomplishment was playing the lead role in reorganizing the PTA and coordinating the development of a new charter that gave the group defined goals to pursue.

List this goal on the left side of a piece of paper and specify the muscles you exercised in accomplishing it on the right side, directly opposite the achievement. For example:

Peak accomplishment	Muscles exercised (specific skills and abilities required)
Led reorganization of PTA and managed group development of a new, more meaningful charter. Obtained school authorities' approval and cooperation.	Leadership ability (persuasive communications and people integration abilities). Good politician in positive sense.
	Motivational skills (sensitive to other people's needs and desires).
	Team building (can recognize others' strengths and organize them into an effective team).
	Delegation skills.
	Problem solving (can sort out key issues and get people working on solutions).
	Administrative skills (can organize, control, and track activities delegated to others and integrate them into final products).
	Negotiating skills (can moderate conflicting views and help a group integrate them into a consensus).

These would be the type muscles I'd exercise in management, community relations, elective office, school administration, or a number of other potential career paths involving people integration, communicating, and interpersonal relations muscles. Clues to which would be best for me should come from the pattern of other peak accomplishments I combine with this.

Suppose, on the other hand, my top peak accomplishments were things like getting a graduate degree in physics, making a breakthrough in the state of the art in my technology, and presenting a well-received paper at the national convention of my professional society.

Skills (muscles exercised) that might surface from identifying these could be:

- Ability to concentrate and master complicated new concepts (fast learning ability).

- Strong technical comprehension and analytical ability.

- Problem-solving abilities (can see patterns in data and focus on core issue.)

- Creativity (ability to combine existing concepts in new ways—or create entirely new concepts).

- Writing skills (can communicate clearly on paper in concise ways that make my points clear).

These would be clues indicating I might enjoy pursuing further graduate work in technical areas and/or doing advanced research and development.

If, by chance, my accomplishments included all the technical, analytical skills above plus reorganizing and leading the PTA, I might consider being a manager—but I'd be wise to look for management of highly technical people in highly technical work.

If my prime accomplishments were organizing the PTA (people interaction muscles) and fulfilling a passion for architecture and remodeling old houses, one possibility would be real estate.

Enough examples. I may be overstructuring your thinking and leading you astray.

Table 11.3 shows a form you can use to analyze specific muscles exercised against each specific peak accomplishment. Table 11.4 contains a laundry list of typical muscles and skills people use in different jobs. You can use this list to stimulate your thinking, but don't limit yourself to it.

Take a piece of paper and run a vertical line down the middle dividing it into two halves. At the top, label the left-hand column "Peak Accomplishments." Label the right-hand column "Muscles Exercised." Now begin your own analysis.

Take your time. Resist the temptation to run the accomplishments together and brainstorm the muscles exercised collectively. That is a dangerous shortcut that may cause you to lose data and insights.

Table 11.3 Identifying preferred skills (muscles exercised in peak accomplishments and things I do well and enjoy—a skill ability inventory)

Instructions

Review your list of most satisfying accomplishments to date. Then prepare a list of the skills and abilities that enabled you to achieve each most satisfying accomplishment (i.e, what intellectual, emotional, interpersonal, analytical, technical, etc., muscles did you exercise in the accomplishment?). This will give you important clues to things you do well.

You may find this a little difficult because our cultural norm is to be modest. In certain situations the cultural norm of modesty makes sense. However, in the context of a career-planning effort, to avoid explicit consideration of your strengths is to court disaster. Career success is a function of strength management, which requires as a minimum strength identification.

Peak experiences (most satisfying accomplishments to date)	Muscles exercised (specific skills and abilities required)

Table 11.3 *Continued*

There may be some important things you feel you do well (and enjoy)
that don't happen to be related to your list of peak accomplishments. If so,
list them below:

Table 11.4   Sample skills

Analytical	Managing
Numerical	Planning
Interpersonal	Organizing
Technical	Communicating
Persuasive	Selling
Measurement	Writing
Integration	Presenting
Artistic	Decision making
Graphic	Teaching
Research	Team building
Clerical	Delegating
Administrative	Negotiating
Financial	Problem solving
Evaluative	Creating

List each accomplishment separately and exhaust the list of muscles exercised on the first one before you go on to number 2. Make a complete list of muscles exercised on number 2 before you go on to number 3 and on down through a minimum of five accomplishments.

If the muscles exercised on each successive accomplishment start to get repetitive, fine; repeat them on each successive accomplishment anyway. That's how this design works. These are precisely the patterns you are looking for.

Above all, do *not*—absolutely do not—allow yourself to think at all right now about which job career path (which door) will allow you to utilize the pattern of muscles and skills emerging from this analysis. That will contaminate and restrict your thinking. We'll worry about what career path this is leading to later. At this point in the process also ignore what jobs are and are not actually available. Concentrate on muscles you want to exercise. Break out of your traditional thinking patterns. Take off the blinders and free form it for a while. There may be possibilities you never dreamed of. At least keep an open mind for now.

When you have finished itemizing all muscles exercised on each peak accomplishment, look for patterns or possible omissions. Is there anything you left out?

There may be important skills you feel you have and enjoy that are not related to your peak accomplishments. If so, list them. "Peak accomplishments" is only a starting point to get your thought processes organized and moving. Fill out your list by adding other muscles (skills/abilities) you like to use.

If you can do so, discuss your list of muscles exercised with someone else. We find in workshops that discussing the data generated with others helps flesh out each individual's thoughts. Discussion fixes any insights gained in your mind better, and adds new dimensions of awareness about them. Your spouse or a close associate may point out muscles you've overlooked.

Review your final list and read on for the next step. We are now moving into step 3 on the roadmap.

Developing generic future job-content objectives (an exercise)

Before I look behind doors and collect data about the content of potential future jobs, I need specific evaluation criteria. Then I can measure the content against these criteria to determine which career paths actually lead in directions I want and which are likely to lead in directions that won't appeal to me.

You've been developing considerable raw data for these criteria. You've isolated your personalized set of most important life values. You've rank ordered these values and made Adult decisions identifying which you might trade off and in what order if faced with an impasse. That's one set of measurement criteria you can use to evaluate future career options.

If a given career path prohibits realization of your two top life values, you'll want to cross it off your list and take some other route.

You've looked at Parent, mentor, and other tapes. You've considered how each might be leading you in nonrewarding directions and analyzed what course corrections may be necessary.

You've looked at peak accomplishments. You've identified muscles and skills you and your Natural Child enjoy exercising most.

A career path that doesn't allow me to exercise those muscles I want to use most is not for me. I won't enjoy it and I'll dissipate my energies.

Table 11.5 shows a form you can use for developing your Generic Future Job-Content Objectives (i.e., criteria) after reviewing the data you've generated in previous exercises.

Look ahead a minimum of five years from now. Do not consider your next job. You need to see the pattern of where you are aiming longer range before you can decide whether or not any next job fits into that pattern.

Consider how you want to be spending your time on the job (your 40–50 hours of work per week) in the future. Don't worry about what jobs will allow this. *Think now only of how you would ideally spend your work time.*

Look first at what muscles you will want to be exercising on the job in the future. Draw your pattern from your peak accomplishments and muscles you've enjoyed exercising most in the past.

Next identify muscles you definitely do *not* want to be exercising 5–10 years from now at work. Look at chores you've disliked in past jobs. We remember these easily, and you should have plenty of data here. Rank order these (most disliked to least disliked).

When you've finished your lists, move on and look at your final life-value card rankings. List your top five values in rank order (most important, next important, etc.). Then list your remaining value cards in the rank order you gave them (ranked 6, 7, 8, 9, etc.).

Table 11.5   Developing Generic Future Job-Content Objectives

---

After reviewing the data you've developed in previous exercises (value ranking, peak accomplishments, muscles exercised in peak accomplishments, other muscles you want to exercise, etc.), develop a consolidated list of Generic Future Job-Content Objectives.

Look ahead a minimum of five years from now and, if possible, as much as ten years. Do not consider your next job. You need to see the pattern of where you are aiming longer range before you can decide whether or not any next job fits into that pattern.

Consider how you want to be spending your time on the job (your 40–50 hours of work per week). Don't worry about what jobs will allow this. Think now only of how you would ideally spend your work time.

Look first at what muscles (intellectual, interpersonal, technical, analytical, emotional, physical, etc.) you will ideally want to be exercising on the job 5–10 years from now. List them below in rank order (most important to least important for you).

Now list what things, if any, you definitely do *not* want to be doing 5–10 years from now at work. Rank order these (most disliked to least disliked).

Table 11.5 *Continued*

Now list your top five identified life values in rank order.

Now list your remaining life values in rank order (6, 7, 8, 9, 10, etc.)

The data on this form will be your consolidated set of specific, personalized, measurement criteria against which you can judge the suitability of any potential future career path for you.

The combined lists you've just completed will now become your basic measurement/evaluation criteria—the standards against which you can compare the actual content of potential future career paths. You can use these to make data-based (not uninformed, shoot-from-the-hip, or guesswork) decisions on which jobs and career paths will lead you in the direction of your maximum possible self-fulfillment. None, of course, will be a total and perfect match; but you can stay in the driver's seat and make your own Adult trade-offs to get the most possible of what's important to you.

If you can, again discuss your final content objectives/criteria with someone else. Mirroring your thoughts with someone else and hearing their reactions is a good self-check on where you are.

Hypothesizing future career possibilities (an exercise)

In our sequence of exercises so far you've been surfacing a great deal of data for your Adult's computer.

Hopefully, much of the data has come from your Natural Child ego state. We've suggested you encourage it to speak up and express itself in a more effective and systematic fashion than it's done before. Prior to this, you may not have been giving your Natural Child much air time. You may have been squelching it as an "immature" intrusion on what some stern Parent tape told you should be a more "grown-up" (perhaps stereotyped, uptight, and dull) approach to life.

Now that you've practiced getting in touch with your Natural Child, we hope you're discovering how valuable it is to your well-being. Stay in tune with your Natural Child from now on. This isn't dangerous, and your Adult can take over at any time to keep you out of trouble.

Remember "Suffer the little children to come unto me"; not some of the more uptight, Critical Parent grown-ups who had frozen their own becoming, engulfed themselves in stereotypes and platitudes, blotted out the here and now realities, turned off their receivers, shut the door on change and improvement, and lost their inborn facility to perceive some of the most exciting events in human history.

Now it's time for your Adult and Natural Child to do some spontaneous, open to any possibility, brainstorming together.

Look at your consolidated list of Generic Future Job-Content Objectives. Hypothesize all possible career paths that might let you fulfill the maximum possible number of your wants 5–10 years in the future.

Do not limit your speculation to your particular company, organization, institution, or even your current professional field of endeavor.

Fantasize that you are going to retire tomorrow and you can spend the rest of your life doing anything you want to do. What might it be? What will let you achieve your top life values and exercise the muscles you most want to exercise?

Assume this retirement is not going to be a retreat into seclusion, inactivity, or muscle atrophication. Assume it's going to be an open door to growth, learning, fun, exciting muscle development, and generation of increased competencies.

Table 11.6 shows a form you can use for this exercise.

Table 11.6   Hypothesizing future career possibilities

Review your Generic Future Job-Content Objectives (i.e., your consolidation of all the data you've generated so far—peak accomplishments, muscles exercised, other things you do and do not want to do in the future, and life-value hierarchy).

Hypothesize what career paths will enable you to achieve the maximum possible number of your wants on the job 5–10 years from now. Get in touch with your Natural Child. Let your Adult and Natural Child brainstorm this with no restrictions. Don't limit your speculation to your current organization, company, or even your current professional field of endeavor.

Be specific, however. List what you feel the position title, organization (if any), and geographical location would be for each possibility listed.

When you make your list be uninhibited. On each possibility you mention, however, be as specific as you can. Write what you feel the position title, organization (if any), and geographic location of each job might be.

I call this hypothesizing because you have no way of knowing if the possibilities you list will really meet your needs until you test them—until you look behind the doors and actually check out the day-to-day job content, challenges, and realities of the jobs mentioned.

Again, get your Adult and Natural Child in dialogue with each other. Brainstorm a list of what longer range (5–10 years out) jobs might fulfill the maximum possible number of your wants and needs, and allow you to avoid the things you don't want to do.

Complete your list before you move on to the next section. If you can, again share and dialogue your results with someone else.

Reality testing 12

Looking behind doors

Now it's time to look behind doors and find out what's really there. Once I have specific evaluation criteria and some hypotheses about where I want to go, the next step is to look beyond myself and collect objective data on what courses of action can get me there. I can now use my Adult to investigate the actual content and challenges of various career paths I've hypothesized. I can use this data to evaluate which possibilities meet my requirements, and strategize how to achieve them.

Sorting into job constellations (an exercise)

Look at your list of hypothetical future jobs. Are they each unique and separate, or are there some patterns? Do some naturally fall together into allied constellations of jobs that are similar or have much in common?

Purify your list. Eliminate any obvious duplications (different titles but the same job). You were brainstorming and we told you not to worry about order or organization then.

Now organize your list. Arrange natural groupings of similar jobs together. Again look for patterns.

In career-planning workshops we list everyone's hypothesized future jobs on chart paper and post this on the walls. Then we look for patterns and arrange the different jobs into natural constellations that fall together.

Working with people in industrial organizations we usually get one constellation that centers around an ultimate goal of top-level multi-functional general-management and corporate-executive positions.

By multi-functional we mean a position managing and integrating the various standard industrial functions (Marketing, Finance, Engineering, Manufacturing, and Personnel). High-level general managers have the managers of these functions reporting to them.

We get other people who want to concentrate on managing Engineering, Manufacturing, Personnel, or Research and Development as an ultimate goal. These people are dedicated to the technology and creativity of these areas. Some see multi-functional management as highly pressured administrative work too distant from the creativity, technology, or end product. General management requires transition into a different constellation of organizing, staffing, financial, and negotiating muscles that don't appeal to them.

Your life and your choice

No one makes value judgments (good or bad) about someone else's preferences. By this time everyone understands we each have our own unique set of Natural Child desires, talents, and best muscles; it's your life and your choice. Any choice is OK if it meets your personal needs. If we all had the same interests it would be a boring and much too competitive world.

We get groups that cluster around artistic pursuits, around teaching, counseling, and social-service work, around Finance, around Marketing, and so on.

We get people who make a clear decision they want to give top priority to investigating possibilities completely outside large organizations. Their interests have included interior decorating, real estate sales, and independent consulting. One technical Ph.D. decided to investigate law (possibly technical patent law).

Some of these are not as far out as they seem. Often the dramatic changes involve active hobbies people have been studying and developing expertise in for years.

One fellow who opened a marina, for instance, had worked in a marina in his youth. He had maintained and developed his interest in boats over the years as a hobby. He knew boat construction. He understood marine engines. He had studied and then taught after-hours advanced power boat courses. He knew dock construction. He made a Natural Child choice when he jumped into this work full time, but it was not a leap into an unknown blue. He did his homework first.

Generating data

If I know nothing about boats and I decide to operate a marina, I need to ask a lot of questions of informed people to find out what knowledge, experience, training, and skills are critical. Then I make an Adult decision if it's worth the effort. If it is, I spend a lot of time studying and developing myself in the required dimensions before I quit my current job and take on the new task. If the data from my interviews leads me to the conclusion it's not worth the effort or I'm not interested, I cross off that door and move on to others until I find one that is worth the effort. That's how I end any impasse of day-dreaming and making no decision because I have no data for a choice.

Gathering data is how I move out of the "which door" impasse, make decisions, and get on with my life and satisfaction.

Many people are at the "which door" impasse, feeling guilty and depressed over their inability to choose and making no effort to reach out and get the data required for new action. Many don't even perceive that lack of data is their problem. They would never make a technical or business decision without collecting and analyzing data, but somehow their Adapted Child believes people are supposed to choose career doors without asking questions. Worse still, maybe their Adapted Child believes people are supposed to wait for someone in authority to tell them what to do. Worse even than that, someone in authority may tell them what to do and send them (unknown to both) down a career path totally at odds with their personal desires and values. When this happens, years later these individuals wonder why they are bored and the authority wonders why they aren't performing. This is not a hypothetical possibility. I can cite case after case.

How do I reach out and collect the data required to generate autonomous (and practical) new choices for me? I definitely do not wait for—or even expect—my manager or someone in Personnel to collect the data for me. If my interests are in things they haven't done, they don't have the data and probably don't know how to get it. Also, they haven't been through the exercise of getting inside my head and figuring out what's uniquely important to me.

Asking successful people

Instead I ask successful people who are currently doing precisely the sort of things I think I'd like to aim for; and I ask more than one.

If I ask three managers of Marketing what they do and how they got there, I'll get three different sets of answers. There will be overlap. If five successful people in a given career field cite one particular skill as important, I can consider that a core skill—but each will have unique insights; each will have put a little different English on his or her strategy for getting there. By comparing them, I can settle on the core requirements and be creative about what unique English I have to make myself stand out.

Personnel and managers (and peers, friends, neighbors, mates, relatives, colleagues, etc.) can help introduce me and set up interviews. *I* will collect and analyze the data.

At first glance, this idea of interviewing successful people in my hypothesized areas of future interest (which are sometimes totally unrelated to what I'm doing today) may seem impractical. Why should they take their valuable and scarce time to talk to me?

Our workshop participants have found, however, that most successful people are not only willing, but flattered; and they thoroughly enjoy the experience of being interviewed like this.

In workshops we establish teams around like interests. They meet and establish a 90-day plan to complete all their interviews. They elect a team leader to coordinate the results and prepare a presentation which they will share with the other teams in a 90-day follow-up session.

The teams use organization directories, personal knowledge, any and all sources to identify successful people to be interviewed in their identified fields of interest. They decide which members of their teams will do each interview. If the person to be interviewed is within reasonable geographic proximity, several members of the team go together and conduct a joint interview.

If the interviewee is at some distant geographic location, they try to identify a team member whose normal business travel takes him or her to that area and this person does the interview.

I've found the teams are very inventive and autonomous at somehow finding ways to interview people all over the country without having their managers complain about increased travel and living expenses. Most people who saw our original program design expressed fears the whole thing would flounder on the cost of conducting the interviews. It didn't happen. Somehow people are motivated enough to find low-cost ways to do the job.

If a person-to-person interview is impossible, the teams assign someone to do it by phone. People predicted high-level executives would never submit to this type of interview with a stranger on the phone. So far we have had almost no refusals and a surprisingly high level of candor in the phone interviews.

Our participants have done phone interviews with nothing more than a brief advance letter to a stranger explaining that they will call and why. We recommend they find someone who knows the interviewee and have him or her pave the way with a preliminary phone call, however.

People enjoy being asked

Actually being interviewed this way is very flattering. It's fun. No one is asking for a job. All they are asking you to do is talk for a while about your favorite subject—you.

Suppose you had an acquaintance call and say a friend was doing some career planning. After much soul-searching this friend had decided a career just like yours might be the most meaningful and self-fulfilling thing he or she could do. The person needed some information, however—such as what the work really consisted of and how to prepare for it. Your mutual acquaintance told this individual you were an expert who could give the best possible answers. Would you talk to this person? No homework is required from you, and the individual is not looking for a job—just advice from an acknowledged expert.

What would you say? Our experience shows people up through very high levels say yes; and feedback shows they have fun in the interview. Sometimes, despite the plan, they also eventually end up hiring the interviewer.

Potential data sources

Table 12.1 is a brief laundry list of potential data sources you can use to stimulate your thinking on how to establish interviews with people in jobs you've identified as of potential interest to you.

Sample job-content questions

Table 12.2 shows some "job-content" starter questions you can use to get the interviews moving when you first meet the interviewees. You

Table 12.1 Reality testing

Potential data sources

- Current incumbents in jobs identified
- Friends who know incumbents and can pave way for you to interview them
- Past incumbents you may know
- Former associates now working in or near organizations, businesses, locations that interest you
- Personnel people in your own or other locations
- Your current manager and former managers
- People your manager can arrange an introduction/appointment with
- Generic or specific job descriptions and candidate specifications in personnel
- Library resources and periodicals describing different industries
- Other managers you know who may be acquainted with areas/jobs that interest you, or who may know someone they can introduce to you

---

Table 12.2 Reality testing

Sample job-content questions

- What is true job content?
- How do incumbents really spend their time in a typical day and week?
- What are true job challenges?
- What do incumbents feel they actually contribute?
- What are typical frustrations in the job?
- What are real satisfactions in the job?
- What muscles (intellectual, emotional, interpersonal, analytical, technical, etc.) does job really require incumbent to exercise?
- Do these match your job criteria?

---

can build creatively on this as opportunities surface during the interviews.

Sample career-progression questions

If the answers to the "job-content" questions show the real challenges of the job meet the personal criteria you established in your Generic Job-Content Objectives, you then move into the second "career progression" part of the interview. Here you collect data on job qualifications for the position in question (i.e., how do I prepare myself to qualify?). Table 12.3 shows some questions you can use to ease the interview into this "career-progression" area.

Table 12.3   Reality testing

Sample career-progression questions

If job-content data verifies your hypothesis that the job meets your job-content criteria—

- What knowledge, skills, or experience in technical, management, or administrative areas is required to qualify for the job?
- What credentials are required?
- What were career paths of successful incumbents?
- What elements/experiences in their career paths were essential to incumbents' success in obtaining and performing in their jobs?
- What elements/experiences in incumbents' career paths were peripheral or unnecessary to success in obtaining and performing in these jobs?
- Which of these key skill/experience requirements do you already possess?
- Which of these key skill/experience requirements do you need to get?

Note:

Move into the "career-progression" section of the interview only if the interviewee's answers to the "job-content" questions show that he or she is in a job of potential interest to you (i.e., the job represents a career path that meets your Generic Job-Content Objectives). If this career path interests you, you need to learn how you can further your qualifications for it. *Remember* you are projecting at least five years into the future.

I recommend you conclude the interview after the "content" questions if answers show the interviewee's job does not meet your job-content criteria. Why go on if you're crossing off that door? You don't have to say this to the interviewee, of course.

Our workshop participants gather data to share with the entire group, so they cover both dimensions of the interview whether or not the "content" questions reveal something personally interesting.

So far our participants' interests have varied enough that no one person in a given organization has been overly burdened with requests to be interviewed.

Outside the organization we'll always have people interviewing the boat captains, artists, candle-shop owners, lawyers, doctors, and real estate people. That's fun. It adds variety. It opens new lives for some—and the list is so varied, no single person is likely to be interviewed to the point of annoyance.

Besides giving you data for making choices and plans, conducting these interviews also gives you significantly increased visibility and a broader circle of colleagues and acquaintances inside and outside your current organization.

This can also contribute a great deal to your autonomy, potency, and ability to expand your options. More about the positive politics of that later.

References

Part 3

Chapter 10

1. Warren H. Schmidt, Lecture on *Dealing with Youth's Changing Values,* delivered at the General Electric Company's Management Development Institute, Crotonville, N.Y., 1971.

2. The response-ability theme was presented by Helene Aronson in one of her 1972 Philadelphia lectures.

Becoming
a winner

Part **4**

Accepting the challenge and succeeding.

Autonomy
is a challenge 13

Joining the doers

So far in this book, our prime concentration has been on goal clarity
—on deciding what you want to do. Until you decide that, you have
nothing to develop an action strategy for.

From here on I'll be presenting data (realities and techniques) on
"how to get what you want." If your Child can finally know what you
want, how can your Adult get the most possible? I'll outline specific
procedures that will help you do that. I'll also describe typical pitfalls
and traps people encounter (or generate themselves) along the way
and recommend approaches for maneuvering around them.

My observation is that most people in large organizations do not
strategize in any systematic way for their own personal growth and
satisfaction.

I'll be talking further about why some do and some don't; and
how, if you so choose, you can join the doers. I'll be pointing out more
strategic career-planning realities with emphasis on how you can work
smarter instead of longer.

It's free choice

When we move into the interviewing, data-collection, and reality-
testing phase of our workshop program, we make a clear shift toward
participant responsibility for the production of end products. The in-
structors back out as course leaders and counselors. We shift the
baton to each individual to act or not act, as he or she chooses. It's
free choice.

Up to the point of reality testing in the workshops—and in this book—we talk about the necessity for individual autonomy and self-direction, but don't test it much. Up to this point, we provide structured exercises and lead people through them. Even at this level, personal commitment and energy are critical factors in how much benefit anyone derives from the experience.

Better-informed decisions

My purpose in this book is not to create new Critical Parent tapes that make people feel guilty if they don't generate active, energetic programs for personal growth. My purpose is merely to define the realities as I see them—to document what my own personal (and fallible) observation has led me to believe are the factors that determine which people do and do not get what they want in terms of satisfaction and self-fulfillment on the job. Hopefully, this will at least help you make a better informed choice on how much energy you want to devote to this objective. This is a very key decision in the career-planning process.

Awareness

Some elect to make the effort, some don't. Either choice is OK. None of us should make any value judgments on which course—active or passive, proactive or reactive—is more or less moral than the other for anyone else. Whatever your decision might be, I do believe that an aware and conscious choice is better than an unaware, nonconscious choice.

Commitment

Taking the initiative to go out on your own—to make contacts, risk being rejected by some, continue despite periodic rejections, conduct interviews, collect data, analyze and strategize to overcome barriers—requires a higher level of energy, motivation, risk, and commitment than anything I've suggested you do so far. You may already be doing this. If you're not, it may be you have other values that are more important to you personally than career planning.

Winners conserve time

If you're typical, taking the necessary steps to do a good job of planning the rest of your career will require improved management of your time. Effective time management is one essential dimension that separates the winners from the losers and the also-rans in the pursuit of career success.

One of the first steps toward turning a great deal of nonproductive time into productive time is to avoid ineffective interpersonal games. Whether or not you decide to invest more time and energy in improved career planning, definitely work at avoiding self-defeating, time-wasting games.

Avoiding nonproductive career games 14

Games dissipate time and energy

One of Berne's most successful books was entitled *Games People Play*. In it he pointed out how most of us dissipate enormous amounts of time and energy playing nonproductive interpersonal games. With games we fill our time busily but nonproductively, futilely waiting for Santa Claus. Avoiding games is one way to stop waiting and start doing.

Berne said games are "sets of ulterior transactions, repetitive in nature, with a well-defined psychological payoff."[1]

By transactions Berne means any communication between people. Ulterior means that the real intent of the transaction is something other than the surface intent presented. In other words, the real intent is devious. This deviousness may or may not be conscious on the part of the transactor. Usually we are not clearly aware of our devious purposes in games. Games have become a habitual process we engage in to fill time while avoiding the tougher realities of more candid and authentic communications.

Games follow a specific sequence as follows:

$$\text{Con} + \text{Gimmick} = \text{Response} \rightarrow \text{Switch} \rightarrow \text{X} \rightarrow \text{Payoff}[2]$$
$$\text{(Confusion)}$$

A typical career-defeating game

One typical career-defeating game is called *Why Don't You—Yes, But*. It follows the sequence shown in Table 14.1.

Table 14.1 Game sequence for *Why Don't You—Yes, But*

Con	+	Gimmick	=	Response →	Switch	→	X	→	Payoff
Ask for advice but don't really want successful advice. Instead want to prove (consciously or unconsciously) that advisor can't handle the situation either and maintain the impasse.		Advisor's weakness. He or she mistakenly believes it's his or her responsibility to solve other people's problems for them.		Advice is given	All suggestions given by advisor are rejected with a repeated "Yes, but . . ." Person ostensibly asking for advice switches to advisor's Child Critical Parent and shows advisor's Child that "You can't handle it either."		Confusion on part of advisor.		Person asking for advice can retreat into favorite negative emotion or racket (e.g., anger or disappointment) and feel satisfied in doing nothing to solve the problem.

Individuals may initiate *Why Don't You—Yes, But* with their managers or personnel representatives repeatedly if they are at a career impasse and avoiding some personal decision required to end the impasse.

They may want challenges not available at their current location and not want to face the necessity of moving to get them. Their Adaptive (or even Natural) Child may be avoiding the fact that they can't have both.

On the other hand, they may be afraid to incur the displeasure of their current manager by asking permission to look elsewhere in the company.

Whatever the decision they are avoiding, they also want to avoid the anxiety involved in not making the decision. They want to share or project the blame elsewhere; and they want to fill their time with something more exciting than worrying.

For these reasons they may go to their personnel representative and initiate the game as follows:

Con

Individual enters the personnel representative's office, explains dissatisfaction with current assignment, and asks for advice. However, the individual doesn't want successful advice. He's at an impasse that requires a decision only he can make. He doesn't want to face that decision. Any advice that brings him closer to the required decision will be rejected. He uses the game to show that the advisor really can't handle the situation either and thus feels justified in doing nothing.

Gimmick

The con hooks into a weakness of the personnel representative. She mistakenly believes it's her responsibility to solve other people's problems for them.

Response

The personnel representative, wanting to help and believing it's her job to do so, gives advice repeatedly. (This, by the way, gives her excitement and fills her time. She's a willing player.)

Switch

All advice is rejected with the equivalent of a repeated "yes, but," thus proving the advisor cannot really help.

For example:

Advice
Why don't you ask your manager for permission to look elsewhere? Have you considered that?

Response
Yes, but my manager is the type who would get angry and feel rejected. He'd hold it against me.

Advice
Why don't you explain that it isn't personal? You've merely outgrown the job. It's our policy to grant permission to look when people want new assignments. Your manager knows that.

Response
Yes, but he'd still feel rejected. I don't know how to avoid that.

Advice
You can point out that your career growth requires exposure to new challenges. Let him participate in the decision on whether or not he can provide new challenges in his group.

Response
But I don't really know what I want to do next.

Advice
Try our career-planning workshop. That would help you clarify your direction.

Response
But I'm busy. I don't have time for that.

The conversation could and probably would go on longer, but you have the idea. Eventually it would result in:

Confusion: The advisor would run out of advice, get confused, and feel angry, disappointed (whatever her favorite and habitual negative emotion was).

Payoff: The person soliciting advice could now also feel anger, disappointment (whatever his favorite negative emotion was) and leave with his decision to do nothing reinforced.

We play games for numerous reasons. Some of these are to do the following:

- *Get strokes* (positive or negative)
- *Structure (fill) our time*
- *Make people predictable* (The person seeking advice in the above game is manipulating the advisor into very predictable responses —including confusion.)
- *Avoid intimacy* (i.e., avoid the more open and direct ways of transacting)
- *Maintain a high level of excitement*
- *Maintain life position* such as "I'm OK—You're Not OK." (More about this later.)

None of the above payoffs are as productive or reality oriented as communications designed to confront needed decisions.

The person asking for advice in the above game vented his frustrations and reinforced his false notion that he was helpless.

The personnel representative absorbed the frustration and reinforced her own feelings of inadequacy and impotence. She goes home and kicks the dog or yells at her kids.

Both have spent a busy but useless afternoon getting nowhere.

Persecutors, Rescuers, and Victims

Steve Karpman, a California psychiatrist who worked with Berne, has identified three basic roles in games (Persecutor, Rescuer, and Victim).[3] The players switch roles as the game progresses. Figure 14.1 shows the Karpman Drama Triangle.

In our *Why Don't you—Yes, But* example, the individual seeking advice began the game in the role of Victim asking for help. The personnel representative readily assumed the role of Rescuer and gave advice.

By repeatedly rejecting the advice the original Victim subtly switched to the role of Persecutor. He demonstrated to the personnel representative that her advice was useless.

Fig. 14.1 The drama triangle (From Stephen B. Karpman, "Fairy Tales and Script Drama Analysis," *Transactional Analysis Bulletin* VI, no. 26 (April 1968), pp. 39–43. Copyright 1968 by the International Transactional Analysis Association, Inc. Reprinted by permission.)

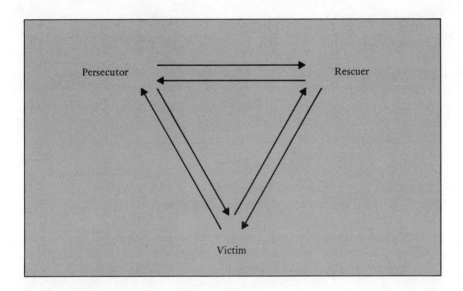

Unknowingly, the original Rescuer (personnel representative) found herself in the role of Victim with no way to rekindle her self-image of competent Rescuer. This doesn't mean there was nothing in it for her, however. She had also filled her time, added some excitement to her day, avoided intimacy and confrontation of the real issue (she couldn't rescue because only the individual could end his own impasse), made people predictable (this is probably a frequent game for her), and so forth. Maybe she often kicks the dog while waiting for her own Santa Claus.

Neither ended the game feeling potent or anywhere nearer solving the problem at hand. That is why games are such a waste.

Other games that defeat career planning are:

- *Ain't It Awful* (We're both helpless, let's convince each other why.)

- *If It Weren't For . . .* _____ (Fill in the blank . . . usually your favorite Victim.)

- *Gee You're Wonderful, Professor* (You solve my problem.) The professor can be my boss, mentor, the system (you decide which).

How do I quit wasting time on game playing? How do I stop starting games or joining in when others initiate a game?

Playing it straight

A straight (as opposed to ulterior or devious) transaction will stop a game. If I don't want to waste time in games, I can look at reality and talk about facts. That takes practice, but it is very rewarding.

Many personnel representatives (and many well-meaning managers) are habitual Rescuers. They believe it's their role to solve other people's problems, as opposed to helping people recognize their own powers to solve their own problems.

I have to watch out for people like this (well meaning as they are) and not let them overly influence me, waste my time, or lull me into a false sense of security (Big Daddy knows best and he'll take care of me). Years later I may find the benevolent manager didn't understand the system either; and his or her advice wasn't worth anything in terms of achieving my values. My only real security is in my Adult awareness and ability to cope with realities myself. Any effective manager or counselor knows that.

The personnel representative could have been much more helpful if she had recognized what was happening and quit giving advice. She could have dropped the Parent/Advisor/Rescuer role and moved into the Adult/Problem Analysis/Facilitator role. She could have shifted the responsibility for action and decision to its rightful owner with Adult questions that required the individual to process his own data (i.e., get into his own Adult and think for himself) as follows:

- What do *you* feel would be the best solution given the facts of your situation as you see them?

- Have you thought about different options for action *you* might develop? What are they? What would the pros and cons of each be in *your* mind?

- What are the risks of asking your manager for permission? What are the risks of not asking? What are the risks to you of no change and leaving things as they are? Have you defined these for yourself? Have you weighed them against the risks of asking for permission and having your manager get angry?

The personnel representative could have taken a different tack. She could have expressed the Process realities of where she was (i.e., what she was thinking and feeling), and asked where the individual was in the Process sense:

> I'm feeling uncomfortable, as though perhaps you don't want my advice or feel it isn't helpful. Is there some way I can be more helpful? What are your reactions to our conversation so far?

Or a more direct approach:

> I'm feeling like we're playing a game called *Why Don't You—Yes, But.* It's a common and nonproductive counseling error. How do you feel? Can we find a more productive approach?

Ways to handle games

There are many ways to handle games: you can play them, but over the long haul that won't get many problems solved; you can ignore them by changing the subject and keeping your own transactions straight, no matter how many invitations to a game the other person issues; and you can confront them by identifying the game for what it is.

All productive ways involve keeping your own transactions straight and reality oriented. Your best bet is to try to hook the other person's Adult by asking a question that requires him or her to present and analyze data. If you succeed he or she will start coming on straight and you can both begin processing real-world data for problem solution or planning.

If you continue with straight transactions despite repeated invitations to do otherwise with someone who refuses to give up game playing, that person will eventually leave you alone and find other game partners.

An adult solution

If you are a manager and people you'd like to help begin to avoid you because you won't play games, you have not failed. You have maintained your own reality orientation and invited them to do the same. That is the most powerful way you can offer assistance. If they refuse, you will prolong their impasse—not help them—by accepting their invitation into games.

If they insist on maintaining their games that is their problem, not yours. You have no obligation to waste your own time because they waste theirs. You can lead a horse to water, but you can't make it drink, and you can't be responsible if it dehydrates standing in front of a pond.

If you are the individual seeking career counseling and your manager or personnel representative won't drop the Rescuer role, and insists on pontificating or avoiding the realities of your unique career needs, calmly but definitely find another horse.

Games are only one of the ways Eric Berne tells us we use our time. Our next chapter looks at other ways.

Finding time 15

Everyone can use time more efficiently

Working smarter instead of longer is time management. Each individual has a finite amount of time at his or her disposal. We can't change that.

We can structure the amount of time we do have. We do structure our time continuously and everyone can do that more efficiently with increased awareness and techniques.

Structuring time

Berne tells us there are six basic ways people structure (fill) their time. These are:

- Withdrawal

- Rituals

- Activities

- Pastimes

- Games

- Intimacy[4]

These six ways are in reverse rank order according to the frequency of strokes and intensity of interactions with other people that each involves. Withdrawal involves the least intense interactions with others (essentially none). Intimacy involves the most intense and authentic interactions with others.

Except for games, which by definition are devious, each of these ways for structuring time can be positive. Each can also be overdone. The goal is to keep them in the right balance to achieve my values.

Withdrawal is isolation from others—a retreat into myself, perhaps into fantasy or remembrance of past strokes. Used judiciously, withdrawal can be used for quiet contemplation and renewal.

Rituals are preset standardized exchanges of recognition strokes (e.g., Hi—How are you?—Fine thanks—See you). Rituals require minimum time, energy, self-disclosure, and commitment.

Activities are work. Activities deal with external facts or realities and result in some product or output. Much of our time on the job is spent in activities (some productive and some nonproductive).

Pastimes are general conversations around specific, usually innocuous subjects such as cars, sports, or the weather. Pastimes are low-risk conversations that reveal very little about the participants personally. In a pastime I can safely test the waters with people, and choose those I might like to know better. Pastimes are popular at cocktail parties.

Games are devious, repetitive, and crooked. Time spent in games is nonauthentic and not really helpful. Games can be exciting because (with the exception of intimacy) they involve more intense interpersonal interactions than the other forms of structuring time.

Intimacy is the absence of other ways for structuring time. Intimacy is authenticity—straight, strong, unguarded, mutual sharing of present realities. Intimacy is caring and allowing ourselves to be vulnerable. In that sense it can be risky, but it is the most rewarding way of structuring time. Intimacy is not excessive or naive sentimentality—and it doesn't necessarily involve sex.

Sex can be the focus for any one of the ways we structure time. Depending on the relationship of the participants, sex can be intimate, a pastime, a game, even an activity (work) for someone who does it for a living.

More authenticity

None of us can spend all our time in intimacy. It isn't practical to be that close to everyone. Almost all of us can spend more time being authentic than we do; and we can selectively expand our circle of intimate acquaintances. All of us can consciously avoid nonproductive games and devious transactions.

Authenticity is risky. It requires acknowledging and sharing realities (pleasant and unpleasant) we might prefer to avoid. Authenticity, however, can be very practical if it encourages us to face into difficult decisions and end impasses.

Mis-structuring time

With the exception of authentic intimacy, all ways of structuring our time can be overdone and become harmful blocks to our growth.

Withdrawals, rituals, activities, pastimes, and games can all be used to avoid realities and perpetuate impasses. This avoidance robs us of critical time our Adult needs to achieve our values.

If my Adapted Child is afraid of the risks involved in facing unpleasant facts, it can tune in some powerful, negative Controlling Parent tapes on "idle hands being the devil's workshop" and load my time with *unnecessary activities* that leave no time for Adult strategizing. I can dissipate large amounts of time playing the game of *Harried* by generating busywork and feeling righteous about my inability to concentrate on achieving my personal life values.

Spending excessive hours passively in front of a TV is a common method of *withdrawing* and not thinking about what I need to do to make my life more interesting.

I can use formalized *rituals* to keep people at a distance and make meaningful dialogue impossible. Office rituals built on authority hierarchies can provide effective vehicles for supervisors to suppress negative feedback that might show them they are off course.

Excessive use of *pastimes* in superficial nonintimate social contacts can help me block out difficult value or decision impasses and keep me busily getting nowhere for years.

Busyness without accomplishment

Busyness and lack of time are the most universally available excuses in the world for avoiding the unpleasant realities of whether or not I am really pursuing my values. Being "too busy" conveniently allows me to decommission my Adult, to avoid decisions, to escape necessary risks and confrontation, to blame all my problems on circumstances, and even to feel noble about my self-imposed impotency.

Everyone can present unanswerable arguments about why lack of time makes living his or her own life in a meaningful fashion impossible. I have never met an exception—and to debate with someone using these arguments is a waste of time. If I choose to use this crutch no one else will convince me I have other choices. I must convince myself I have other options and make a personal decision to create them. If I dehydrate standing in front of a pond, that choice (conscious or unconscious) is mine also. Busyness creates a lot of dehydration in this world.

How to overcome busyness (an exercise)

I have met people who consciously decided to quit availing themselves of their busyness excuse: to face facts, set priorities, eliminate the nonnecessary activities, and make time to get on with the business of living their lives the way they want to.

One way to start doing this is to monitor your time for two weeks, hour by hour. Use the format shown in Table 15.1. Three times a day (at lunch, at quitting time, and at bedtime) take ten or fifteen minutes to make notes on what specific things you did under each of the ways to structure time since your last note session. If you have a secretary, have him or her keep a record minute by minute of your working day and then translate these notes to the form shown in Table 15.1. A common desk-top calendar with tear-off sheets showing each day's schedule can also be useful for recording notes.

As your list develops, look for patterns. Analyze the patterns and be honest with yourself. What was really necessary and useful? What could you have eliminated? What was really required to earn a living and maintain your family's welfare? What were the frills?

Which of the things you spent time on moved you further toward realizing your life values? Which were meeting archaic Parent, mentor, or other injunctions? What were unnecessary efforts to impress other people who don't need to be impressed (or who aren't even interested enough to notice)?

Which of the actions recorded were unproductive avoidance behavior—time fillers to keep you from facing an impasse, or a neces-

Table 15.1 Time analysis chart

Time	How time was spent	Way time was structured	Real necessity for achieving an important value	Real usefulness in achieving an important value
(e.g., 8:15 to 9:25 A.M.)	(Specific actions such as day-dreaming, eating, meeting on agency report, writing sales letter, discussing weather with associates, playing with kids, etc.)	(Withdrawal, ritual, activity, pastime, game, or intimacy)	(Scale of 1- not necessary to 10- essential)	(Scale of 1- not useful at all to 10- extremely useful)

sary risk? How much time was spent in procrastination avoiding parts of your job that are boring or unnecessary? What can you do about that?

Use your Adult to identify and eliminate the needless time wasters. Look at any high-ranked life values you are not achieving and use the time you salvage to strategize what you can do to start achieving them.

Get out your value cards. Re-sort them using new criteria. This time don't rank them according to the values you want to achieve. Look at your time records and rank them according to how much time you actually devoted to each value (most time devoted to least time devoted). How does the ranking compare to the way you ranked each value's importance to you? Are you devoting too much time to some values that are not important to you? Whose values are they?

Are some important values being neglected? Why? What will you now do about that? Use your Adult to plot a new course.

Eliminate all unnecessary withdrawals, rituals, activities, pastimes, and games that are taking time away from your important values.

Plot a new course for getting more of what you want.

Winners
and losers 16

Creative mistakes

Misuse of time is one of several possible mistakes we've discussed in career planning. Noticing our mistakes, admitting them, analyzing precisely what we are doing wrong, and using the data gained from this analysis as clues to how we can improve our approach next time is a key winner's reaction sequence when setbacks occur. Losers more often tend to blot out or deny mistakes, and blame setbacks on factors outside themselves. Winners have somehow learned that mistakes, if analyzed, can be major building blocks for growth.

I can never be a loser if I learn from my mistakes

One summer I met a priest in the swimming pool at the Goulding's T.A. Institute. He was back for his second summer session. He told me about several exciting projects he'd started in the year since his first session, projects he had been reluctant to commit himself to before. He told me why he was able to do them now, and I'll always remember his explanation. It was very simple. He said:

> I learned from the Goulding's last year that I can never be a loser
> if I learn from my mistakes. That changed my whole life. Now
> I'm doing all the things I used to be afraid to try.

It wasn't a new concept to me. I'd said the same thing in lectures myself; but that was the first time I'd really heard it in all my ego states (a bull's eye), and honestly applied it to myself. I don't know

159

why it took hold in me then and not before. Maybe it was a warm pool. Maybe it was the fact that a priest was saying it—a priest frolicking around in the water alternating between his Nurturing Parent and Natural Child—a priest doing exciting things and having fun. (My Child's concept of priests and ministers had been very Controlling Parent up to then).

You don't have to be perfect

Whatever the reasons, that was the first time I successfully broke into and interrupted the ongoing, debilitating Controlling Parent/Adaptive Child dialogue inside my head. That was the first time my Nurturing Parent and Adult broke through to my Child and communicated that:

> It really is OK to make mistakes. You don't have to be perfect . . . honest . . . and you can even *remember* it's OK!

I received the message with mixed emotions. If I admitted I'd been trying to be perfect, I was admitting an imperfection. I also had to recognize the wasted energy and lost enjoyment my "be perfect" injunction had caused during my life to date. My Adapted Child wanted to blot out that idea and assure me those years had indeed been perfect. It took a strong Adult and lots of practice to keep this new admission and insight in my awareness, to realize my whole life to date had been not wasted but merely imperfect—and that that was OK.

I've learned that my Adapted Child exaggerates danger a lot. My Adapted Child sees things as black and white—perfect or a total loss. I have to use my Adult to see my progressively improving shades of gray.

Winners are very imperfect

Winners are very imperfect. If I try to be perfect, I'm going to be a loser.

Nobody likes to make mistakes but everybody does. One thing that distinguishes winners from losers is how they handle mistakes.

Berne defines a winner as:

A person who sets out to do something he *decides to do* and gets it done if it's possible. *If he doesn't get it right the first time, he gets it right the next time.* * (italics added)

A winner realizes that mistakes, when we admit them, are powerful learning opportunities. They lead to new insights and growth.

My Adapted Child, if it's listening to an unreal Parent tape, may try the impossible task of being perfect all the time.

My Adapted Child may be so frightened of being imperfect that it denies the reality of my errors. When it does that it robs me of the learning opportunities in my mistakes. Because I don't learn, I make the same mistakes over and over again, and I quit growing. People who are learning from their errors pass me by, or at least find more personal growth and fulfillment. Because I waste energy denying or avoiding mistakes I have less energy for new risks, new decisions, and new enterprises that will broaden my world and lead to greater success.

Berne tells us winners know what they'll do if they don't succeed on something but they don't talk about it.† In other words, winners look realistically at the fact that a certain percent of the time they'll fail, and failure doesn't destroy them. Winners have their back-up contingency plans in place beforehand. They know how they'll learn from the failure.

Berne tells us losers will talk about what they'll do if they succeed, but they don't know what they'll do if they don't succeed.‡ There are no contingencies. The thought of not succeeding is too unpleasant to contemplate.

Winners usually have more failures than losers

Failure is much more frightening to a loser than it is to a winner. As a result, winners often have more failures on their records than losers do. Winners usually attempt more. They take more risks and make

---

* From Eric Berne, *Sex in Human Loving*, p. 215. Copyright © 1970 by the City National Bank of Beverly Hills, California. Reprinted by permission of Simon & Schuster, Inc.
† Ibid., p. 141.
‡ Ibid., p. 141.

more decisions. People who can't allow themselves to make and admit mistakes don't attempt much. If I don't attempt much I don't fail often, but I don't do much either.

Winners don't waste time defending bad decisions, and bad decisions don't destroy their self-confidence or willingness to make new decisions.

Winners don't become immobilized trying to make all their decisions fail-safe either. They collect as much data as they can knowing there will never be enough time or data to make all decisions perfect. They decide anyway, and they anticipate matter of factly that they'll have to make numerous course corrections as new data reveals some of their decisions were wrong. Waiting to make the perfect fail-safe decision can lead to no decision at all—another impasse.

Winners not only realize being imperfect and making mistakes is the road to success and self-fulfillment; they also realize it's impossible to please everyone. No matter what you do, someone is not going to like it.

A tough balancing act

My Adult tracks reality like a high-wire artist follows a thin line from pole to pole. It's a tough balancing act.

Fall one way, and you enter the pitfall of listening so much to your own and others' Controlling Parent and Adapted Child tapes you do nothing on your own. You spend all your time at the impossible task of trying to please everybody (the voices in your head and the people around you).

Fall the other way, and you blot out all criticism, even the objective data that's telling you you've made a mistake and how to correct course.

A competent computer

Fortunately, my own Adult ego state provides me with a very competent computer to help me keep my balance. My Adult can sort the wheat from the chaff. It can process all the data, calibrate the probabilities, and track that line to where I want to go. My Adult can notice which ego state others are coming from in their transactions with me. Using my Adult I can decide when I'm getting feedback on reality and when I'm getting someone else's archaic Parent or Child tapes. I can notice; I can even predict who will and will not be pleased by a specific decision. I can be choosy about whom I care about pleasing. I can decide to please me. Remember, a winner sets out to do something he or she decides to do. I define winning for me and then use my Adult to track that unique, one of a kind, narrow line to my personal goal.

A zig-zag course

It's a narrow line, but it won't be a straight line. Winners follow a zig-zag path to growth. They are constantly correcting course.

One simple analogy to following a zig-zag path to my goals is the thermostat on a furnace (see Fig. 16.1). My Adult is my thermostat. It and my Natural Child set a goal (70 degrees). My Adult then establishes parameters and feedback mechanisms to let me know when I am or am not on course. When the temperature gets out of bounds (out of the parameters I set) one way (67 degrees) the thermostat turns on the heat to get back on target. When the temperature gets out of bounds the other way (73 degrees) the thermostat shuts off

Fig. 16.1 Thermostat

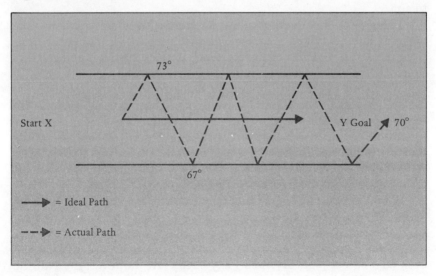

the heat. This zig-zag course, corrected by perception and processing of new incoming data, keeps the temperature within reasonable proximity of my goal. With no thermostat or data processor monitoring reality, the temperature could fall to zero with no alert to the furnace. I could freeze to death. Many are freezing to death with respect to their careers.

Computers need goals

It isn't enough to have a data processor, however. As we've been saying, I also need goals (i.e., need to know where I want to go). Data processors and goals go together.

An analogy here would be the use of computers to keep spacecraft successfully on course. The spacecraft is aimed at a specific target (the Moon or Venus). Data continually sent back from the spacecraft tell the computer where it is at any given moment. The computer makes corrections to keep it on course. The trip to the Moon or Venus is always a zig-zag (on course/off course) one but the spacecraft eventually gets there.

If I have no goal—if I shoot the spacecraft off without knowing whether I want it to go to Mars, Venus, the Moon, or Jupiter, the computer is useless. It can tell me where the spacecraft is but can make no course corrections without some specific destination at which to aim.

Plugging in a computer on a spacecraft with no destination—like plugging in an Adult on a career plan with no goal—is a waste of time.

We need a goal and computer which notices mistakes and corrects course.

Why isn't everybody finding personal growth and satisfaction in his or her work? Some don't have goals. They have no criteria for recognizing satisfaction when they see it. Some have their computers turned off by an overpowering Controlling Parent or Adapted Child that contaminates their Adult and won't let them perceive realities that conflict with outdated tapes (shoulds)—or that activates archaic, no longer relevant, action-inhibiting fears.

Some just don't give a damn about on-the-job growth or achievement. They'd rather do the minimum amount of work required for survival and spend most of their time fishing or bowling. That's OK too—if it's conscious, deliberate, and what they really want. That can even be a career plan. Even as I say that's OK, however, my Natural

Child jumps in and says "Why not work in a marina or a bowling alley?" My Natural Child knows someone who did that, at high risk at age 50. He found a way to own a marina and have a ball.

Winners are planful marketeers

The final step, after winners have defined their career goals, examined them to make sure they will meet their personal criteria for success, and taken a clear look at what they need to do to qualify for the careers selected is to strategize very carefully and consciously how to market their strengths and get the type of jobs that will give them the most valuable experience.

References

Part 4

Chapter 14

1. From Eric Berne, *What Do You Say After You Say Hello?* (New York: Grove Press, 1972), p. 23. Reprinted with permission.
2. Ibid., p. 23.
3. From Stephen B. Karpman, "Fairy Tales and Script Drama Analysis," *Transactional Analysis Bulletin* VII, No. 26 (April 1968), pp. 39–43. Copyright 1968 by the International Transactional Analysis Association, Inc. Reprinted by permission.

Chapter 15

4. From Eric Berne, *What Do You Say After You Say Hello?* (New York: Grove Press, 1972), pp. 21–25. Reprinted with permission.

Market strategies

Part **5**

Using the research to become a
fail-safe candidate.

The next step 17

A tactical decision

Once I've selected a career direction, the next step is to look at my current job. Is it leading me to where I want to be five years from now? Am I:

- Well placed on a steep learning curve that's still teaching me things I need to know to move in directions I choose?

- On the right path but in a flattening out or declining learning curve where I've got all there is to get from this job, things are becoming repetitive, and it's time to seek out the right new growth experience?

- On the wrong path altogether?

Whichever it is, I have to make a tactical decision about when (now or later) it will be time for my next growth step, and what new job or experience that change should involve.

Filling the gaps

If I've done my homework, I've identified what strengths I have to help sell myself. I also know what experience/learning gaps I must fill in if I am to move toward and qualify for my long-range career goal.

My next job experience should be carefully chosen to fill in one of these gaps, and I'll need to sell myself for a job that will do this.

In a world where competition is intense, I'll develop a better personal sales strategy if I first understand the realities of how managers hire.

169

How
managers hire 18

Fail-safe candidates

Several years ago a sampling of managers was studied to determine what criteria they really used in selecting people for key positions. A clear and not surprising pattern emerged—AS MUCH AS POSSIBLE, THE MANAGERS WANTED THE CANDIDATES THEY SELECTED TO BE FAIL-SAFE.

> A large majority (69%) did feel that the appointee's success or failure on the new job could have considerable effect on their own (the appointing manager's) reputations or careers.[1]

Hiring managers are human. Like everyone else, each has an internal, scared Adapted Child. No one wants to fail. If a key subordinate I selected fails to perform in a visible position, I share in that failure.

> The process of selecting the right person to fill a managerial opening appears to be a process of risk reduction. . . . The manager reduces this risk . . . by appointing a candidate whose performance he has had an opportunity to observe in the past.[2]
>
> PERSONAL KNOWLEDGE OF THE CANDIDATE'S PAST PERFORMANCE HAS GREAT INFLUENCE ON THE DECISION PROCESS[3]

> In about three quarters of the selection decisions studied . . . the man selected had either worked for the manager in the past, had worked as a peer, or had worked in the same component closely enough that the manager had been able to observe his performance.[4]

170

Both who *and* what you know

So what's new? The same old game of politics? We knew that all along. It's not "what" you know, it's "who" you know. Right?

No. Not right at all. In fact, very wrong. The *"what"* you know is very important. Who I know is irrelevant unless those "who's" have reason to believe I'm competent. *"Performance"* is critical.

> What may appear from a distance to be politics and favoritism when selections to key positions are made (sometimes referred to as "management by crony") may actually be merely the attempt to reduce risks of failure when the appointing manager alone must bear the responsibility of a poor decision.[5]

Remember, the basic criterion is to reduce the risk of failure. I don't reduce this risk by hiring a crony I know is incompetent; I reduce it by hiring proven competence.

A predictable sequence

Combining documented research with my personal observations of hiring managers over the years, I've concluded managers follow a fairly predictable sequence in seeking a fail-safe candidate.

In recent years the risk of not having a sufficient number of women and minority employees at all levels has been great enough that, happily, considerable effort is put into identifying minority and women candidates at all steps in this sequence.

1. Managers look for someone they personally know can't fail— ideally, someone they have personally observed successfully meeting challenges similar to those in the open job. This doesn't always offer a great deal of challenge or growth to the individual identified, but it is a fail-safe solution for the manager.

2. If this ideal candidate can't be found (or won't accept the job), managers then look for someone they have personally observed meeting lower-level but related challenges. The new job represents some stretch, but managers know the individual well enough to feel comfortable he or she can stretch successfully.

3. If neither of the above personally known candidates can be found, managers then ask close friends and colleagues (people whose judgment they trust) to recommend candidates.

4. Managers will then (and Affirmative Action Programs now usually require this) seriously consider the resumes of unknowns submitted from outside or by the organization's formal employee inventory system.

Even when policy forces review of a candidate slate prepared by Personnel, managers will still go through steps 1, 2 and 3, and then ask Personnel to include candidates they've identified through personal contact on the slate.

Inventory systems

Managers go to inventory and recruiting systems for paperwork on unknowns because:

- They can't identify enough known candidates.

- Organizational policies require them to look at inventory candidates in addition to candidates they have personally identified.

- They have some personal candidates identified but want to check the marketplace on the off chance they can do better.

This isn't cynicism or negative politics. It's merely the basic human tendency to feel more comfortable and less at risk with the known than with the unknown. This doesn't make it ideal or even productive—but it does make it understandable.

People who know people

After reviewing the resumes submitted in step 4, managers will narrow them down to a reasonable number for in-depth research. Then they will immediately start checking out personal friends and associates who might know the identified candidates well enough to give a good "reading" on them.

With regard to information about the candidates available to the selecting manager, the most often mentioned was *reference information from previous managers and associates* (83%).[6]

Even in the case of references, the data showed that 96% of the reference sources contacted were known either personally or by reputation to the appointing manager.[7]

Strategy options

Faced with the above realities, I have choices to make:

- I can denounce the system as negative politics and devote my energies to nonproductive sessions of *Ain't It Awful* with other *Ain't It Awful* players who would rather denounce than cope.

- I can avoid *Ain't It Awful* and devote the energy (and time) thus liberated to productive coping.

Using my Adult, I can recognize the normal human dimensions of the selection process, analyze them dispassionately (if not approvingly), and generate conscious options to use these realities very ethically to my personal advantage.

Understanding that visible candidates (if competent) have the edge, I can deliberately and systematically work at becoming visible to people who have influence in the selection process. In this way, I am more likely to be selected for work that will lead toward my predetermined personal career goals.

After looking at the research, I asked one influential corporate manpower consultant what he was going to do in the future to cope with the facts revealed.

He said he wouldn't change his approach at all. Nothing in the research surprised him. He simply devoted his energies to helping high-potential talents become visible in parts of the company where they wanted to grow.

Sometimes he did this by having them interviewed in situations where he knew they wouldn't get the job simply so they could be met and remembered by the interviewers. He said that if sent back into the same environment six months later, these individuals would have significant advantages over candidates the interviewers had never met. Because they were slightly more known, the risk would be slightly reduced.

Visibility
good and bad 19

An essential asset for performers

Visibility is an asset, of course, only when it reveals competence. Visible incompetence scares potential employers off, particularly my best friends if they think I might ask them for a job.

Apparent contradictions to this do not tend to hold up when we look beneath the surface at what's really happening.

All of us can cite examples of people we've seen in high-paying jobs who weren't competent. I've seen many of these over the years. Almost always they got there through someone else's mistake. Someone who erroneously believed they were competent—managers are not always the world's best evaluators—put them there.

If such an individual and his or her manager have become friends, the manager often, admittedly, finds it difficult to face the situation when the incompetency surfaces, as it inevitably must. At the same time, he or she usually also finds it very risky to leave an incompetent with any real power or decision-making authority. The manager may compromise by letting the individual maintain status, income, even an impressive title—but the real decisions subtly shift elsewhere. If times are good, incompetents can hang in (usually unhappily) for a long time to no one's real advantage, least of all their own. Raises slow down or stop. The boss becomes uncommunicative and difficult to reach. The job becomes boring. The situation is uncertain and scary.

While I've seen managers maintain incompetents on the payroll because they found it too unpleasant to face the situation, I've never seen a manager voluntarily take recognized incompetents along when he or she is promoted.

When a manager moves on or up, the organization breathes a sigh of relief and expects all the cronies to move along too. Not so. Only a few competent cronies move on. It's the departing manager who breathes the sigh of relief, grateful to be unburdened of any cronies who weren't performing. They get left behind for the new manager to handle, and any safety the nonperformers had in their powerful friends deteriorates rapidly.

It's less fatiguing to be competent

Incompetents don't always get fired but neither do they get much challenge, growth, fun, or even any internal feelings of security on the job. It's easier, safer, and far less fatiguing to be competent. Depending on "friends" is risky. They might topple themselves, drop dead, or decide it's too risky to stay friends. The only real security lies in being competent and in making sure people, many people, particularly people who can influence my career, *know* I am competent.

"Who" and "what" you know are both essential.

> Thus, it appears that a young man who is eager to move ahead in the company might be wise to put himself in positions where his performance could be personally observed by the largest number of potential managerial "selectors."[8]

The above, of course, assumes that my performance will be good, a point too often overlooked by the *Ain't It Awful* players who see only the "who you know" side in the two-dimensional "who" and "what" formula for success.

To come out a winner in the selection process I must perform successfully *and* be visible. The more visible I am—the more people who know my talents and can honestly recommend me—the greater my chances of getting the work and career progress I want in a fail-safe-oriented marketplace.

Resumes

None of the preceding discounts in any way the importance of developing a good, sales-oriented resume for inclusion in my organization's personnel inventory system, and for use in periodically sampling the market in outside organizations.

I have never seen anyone hired strictly on their paperwork, but I've seen hundreds rejected on poorly prepared paperwork, often at very high levels in the organization.

Busy executives don't have time for personally interviewing large numbers of candidates. Given 15 resumes, they'll quickly eliminate 10 and narrow down their consideration to the 5 who look best on paper.

A self-defeating circle

Not maintaining a well-written resume in my organization's personnel inventory system can lead to a self-defeating circle of events. I don't get interviewed because my paperwork is poor. Because I don't ever get interviewed, I assume the system is worthless—so the next year I again submit hastily prepared, low-quality paperwork. Where does it end? By remaining in passive ignorance I assure myself of never finding out. Another corner of my own making. More about resumes later.

Assault on
the iceberg 20

Which iceberg?

If the iceberg pictured in Fig. 20.1 illustrates all available jobs in my chosen career field, I can pretty safely assume that only about 20 percent are filled from a slate of candidates all of whom are unknowns in the hiring organization. The other 80 percent are filled from slates containing some candidates who are known to some degree (and are therefore of lower risk) to the hiring managers. I have no proof of this 80–20 ratio, but I've talked with many recruiting experts and this figure generally represents their experience, particularly concerning the key higher-level white-collar openings.

The above, of course, is no surprise if we consider the research on how managers hire. Managers really don't want much cold paperwork on complete unknowns.

Even executive-search firms that recruit full time bypass almost all the unsolicited paperwork they are besieged with, and use the phone and personal contacts to find candidates.

How do I become a known, low-risk candidate on the iceberg of my choosing? How do I make certain my name leaps forward in the minds of people most likely to influence the selection of candidates when a job I want opens up?

The first step is to choose my iceberg carefully. The ocean of career opportunities is crowded with many icebergs, far too many for any one individual to investigate them all (see Fig. 20.2).

Here again, as in our "which door" phenomenon, the first critical step toward success and effective concentration of energy is focus. If I don't zero in and concentrate on one or a few key icebergs, I'll get

Fig. 20.1 The iceberg (of available jobs in my chosen field)

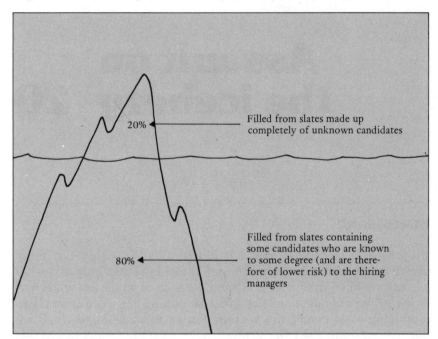

to know and understand none well. If I scatter my attention and energies across all possible icebergs, I'll become known in none well. Leaving all doors open is a nonchoice. I'll get swept through one by chance and find myself riding the wrong iceberg, drifting in directions I don't want to go.

In earlier chapters we outlined specific techniques for detecting your drift and focusing your attention on those icebergs most likely to satisfy you.

Marketing proposals

Assuming now that I have my sights set on the right iceberg, how do I climb aboard? How do I tap into that 80 percent below the surface?

If I've done my research, I know what the most likely requirements are for success on my iceberg. I also know which of the qualifications I already have, and what new job experiences I need to round out my credentials further.

Fig. 20.2 Which iceberg?

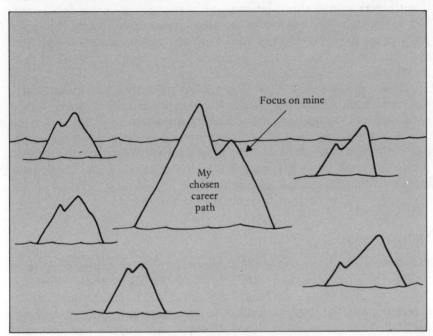

I look at the organizations most likely to offer my desired kind of job, and I work at becoming known in them independent of any current openings. I identify the locations, businesses, organizations, and managers who have the jobs I want and I carefully strategize a multiple assault.

I begin by preparing a carefully worded resume, using the specific vocabulary most likely to be understood and accepted by the people doing the hiring, highlighting those specific aspects of my background most likely to be marketable in my target organizations.

This requires homework—careful research through reading or personal contacts of the target organization, its objectives, needs, challenges, and business vocabulary—so that I can tailor my resume accordingly, and make relevant responses in any personal or interview contacts.

Most of us don't bother to do this homework. Most of us write one quick resume that's supposed to attract all possible buyers. Because it makes sense to us we expect it to appeal to everyone. We fill it with buzz words, abbreviations, and acronyms understandable only to someone who has worked in the same organizations or on the same projects we have. We then sit back with the "arrogance of the expert" and assume it's the readers' problem if they don't understand our shorthand.

The "arrogant expert" who won't take the time to communicate in understandable English has a loser's perspective. Some simple questions help put things back into correct perspective.

Whose problem is it when hiring managers discard resumes that don't communicate? Who has the most to lose? Who loses the opportunity for a job he or she wants? Who is left rejected and not knowing why? Who caused the rejection?

Multiple rewrites

I've seen winners rewriting their resumes 10 or 15 times, preparing several revisions designed (truthfully) to highlight those different aspects of their experience homework shows will be most appealing to different potential organizations. I've seen winners carefully seeking feedback from managers, personnel people, and anyone else who will read their resume to aid in multiple rewrites.

One clever tactic winners sometimes use is to seek out friends, former associates, or friends of friends in their target organizations. They ask these people to critique a resume or make suggestions for rewrite that will make it more marketable in that organization's climate. This, of course, serves multiple objectives. It increases visibility (that critic becomes aware of me as a candidate), develops support and more mutual ownership of my objective (people are more likely to recommend and sell someone whose career move they've helped strategize than a stranger), and helps me write a better marketing proposal (resume).

It helps if I think of my resume as a formal marketing proposal for my most valuable commodity—me.

Everyone knows you have to put this kind of effort into a marketing proposal for a product. Few of us realize the same sort of effort must go into marketing our personal resumes. It's useful for my Adult to notice that some of the competing candidates are putting this level of effort into their paperwork.

Becoming fail-safe

Assuming I now have a well-written, understandable, and persuasive resume, it's still a cold piece of paper to anyone who doesn't know me. How do I warm it up? How do I become more visible and less of a risk as a candidate in my target organizations? I make a multiple assault. I get my carefully tailored resume into the hands of as many residents on that iceberg as possible. I find ways to phone, meet, and talk to everyone I can there. I use all avenues of access I can find to establish my visibility in key places; and I persist inventively and tirelessly, sometimes in the face of indifference and repeated rejection.

One assault wave seldom establishes a beachhead. I've seen determined candidates focus on a target and persist in their assault as much as a year (in one case two years) before scoring a significant hit. Six months is a fairly standard minimum. In the more lengthy efforts the individuals had a clear, well-articulated value at stake or they never would have persisted.

Different avenues of access to targeted organization(s) would include such things as:

- Contacting former managers, peers, or school associates who work there and asking them to critique my resume, get the final version into the hands of the right people, talk about me, make personal inputs on my skills, and stay alert for opportunities.

- Contacting friends who work there and asking the same of them.

- Having my current manager contact people he or she knows there (assuming my manager has agreed to my search and is willing to recommend me).

- Having my personnel manager refer me to the target organization's personnel people with an appropriate endorsement of my capabilities.

- Asking friends who don't work there to contact any friends they might have who do work in the target organization to recommend me.

Multiple access

Visible competence is the key to becoming a low-risk candidate, and multiple access is the key to making my competence visible in that

critical 80 percent of the iceberg below the surface where most of the
real action takes place (see Fig. 20.3).

The more points of contact I have in the target organizations, the
higher the probability I'll score a hit when the type of job I want
opens up. The more people I have recommending my competence, the
greater my competitive advantage over the lesser-knowns.

Fig. 20.3 Multiple access

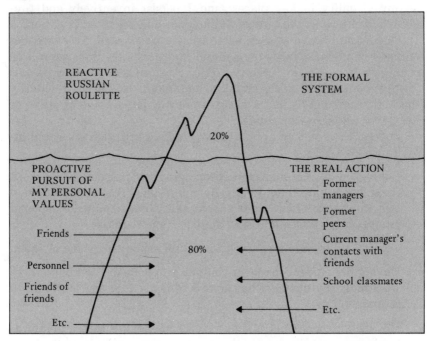

Waiting passively for the formal system to advance my career by
placing me in one of the jobs that surfaces on the top of the iceberg
is like playing Russian Roulette. I may never score a hit. Or even
worse, relying on chance I may score a hit on the wrong iceberg and
drift away from my real needs and values for years without knowing
what's wrong.

The many possibilities for multiple access on the iceberg I choose
multiply rapidly once I consciously and systematically begin to identify them. The proper sequential timing of my contacts, a personalized

approach tailored to the specific contacts, tact, finesse, good salesmanship, and so forth are important if I'm to avoid the overkill of a mass mailout. I want to communicate that I'm competent, interested, and potentially available, not desperate. I can usually trust my Adult ego state to strategize that and learn profitably from any mistakes made, once I consciously charge my Adult with that responsibility.

A case history

One inventive individual I know

- established a career path he wanted to follow.

- identified organizations (inside and outside his company) that offered the right type of work.

- rank ordered the organizations according to their desirability as places to work.

- began by rehearsing his resume, assault tactics, and interview techniques with the least desirable outside places.

- evaluated the results and learned from his mistakes.

- sharpened his sales techniques.

- moved in with his perfected approach on the organizations that most appealed to him.

The confidence he was able to build from his practice (and the viable alternative options he'd generated outside) put him in a position where he could face the opposition of his current manager, act despite it, and generate a very attractive new option for himself inside his own company.

Sometimes, despite all the well-meaning personnel policies to the contrary, we have to generate good visibility and viable options elsewhere before we can take on the economic risk of addressing an obstacle or breaking out of an impasse in our own organization. Sometimes we have to go all the way. Large companies are full of top-level people who broke through an impasse and got what they wanted by quitting, establishing a visible reputation elsewhere, and then returning at a higher level to do what they wanted to do and couldn't.

Reality testing is a key market strategy

One of the best door openers for establishing contacts and visibility in new places is, of course, the very process I've already been through in interviewing successful incumbents to collect data for developing my career-path focus and strategy. The very same strangers who met me, got to know me, counseled me, and helped me strategize my selection of an iceberg now live on that iceberg, probably in key positions influencing what people are brought aboard.

The data-gathering interview is an excellent multiple-purpose tool for collecting facts, selecting doors, and establishing my visibility with people who can help me. In this relaxed, mutual exchange of information situation they'll probably get to know me even better than they would in the more tense interview situation where I'm asking for a job and they face the decision of saying yes or no.

As a process, the data-gathering interviews are practical, effective, energy conserving, straightforward, honest, informative, and fun. They not only help me choose doors, they also help me open doors.

Other methods for establishing my visibility include getting assigned to task forces and special-project teams working on visible issues, professional association contacts, publishing papers or books, and giving presentations at professional gatherings of people in my field. Once I recognize the need, my Adult and Natural Child can collaborate ingeniously to generate all the creative visibility options I need.

References

Part 5

Chapter 18

1. From G. A. Bassett and H. H. Meyer, "A Study of the Personnel Selection Decision Process," *Personnel Practices, Personnel and Industrial Relations, Summary Report,* 1968, p. 3. Reprinted with permission.
2. Ibid., p. 7.
3. Ibid., p. 5.
4. Ibid., p. 5.
5. Ibid., p. 9.
6. Ibid., p. 2.
7. Ibid., p. 8.

Chapter 19

8. Ibid., p. 9.

Successful negotiations

Part 6

Expanding my repertoires for persuasion.

Win-win
dialogues 21

Something for both sides

I've said that career success requires a series of ongoing negotiations between me and other people to achieve my career goals. The other person is usually someone I want to purchase my services or product. The negotiations might be between me and my current manager, me and a prospective hiring manager, me and a client if I work for myself, or me and a customer if I sell a product.

A negotiation gets the best results if it is conducted on a quid pro quo basis. There should be something in it for both sides. With an organization I negotiate so that I can contribute to the organization's goals and at the same time continue to further my own goals on some reasonable timetable. We respect each other's needs and see them as legitimate.

In T.A. terms, the best negotiations are conducted on an "I'm OK-you're OK" assumption. A not-OK assumption on either or both sides raises barriers to success and satisfaction.

This brings us to the concept of life positions and how they affect our ability to negotiate for achieving personal values.

Four positions

Tom Harris, expanding an earlier Berne discovery, explains that each of us is operating from one of four possible life positions at any given point in time.[1] These are:

- I'm not OK-You're OK

- I'm not OK-You're not OK

- I'm OK-You're not OK

- I'm OK-You're OK

I'm not OK-You're OK is the position of the helpless, inexperienced small child dependent on parents and other powerful big people for his or her very survival. When I'm grown up myself, of course, I am one of the big people but my Adapted Child still feels powerless and I feel powerless compared to others when I'm in my Adapted Child ego state.

The *I'm not OK-You're not OK* position is the most despairing of the four. In that position, with no one OK, I feel like giving up and I lose interest in living.

I'm OK-You're not OK is the distrustful position of people who feel persecuted by others. Criminals often operate from this position. The badly battered child frequently assumes this position as one way to survive intolerable mistreatment.

I'm OK-You're OK is, of course, the healthiest and most productive position. In this position I acknowledge my own worth, respect the worth of others, and operate on the assumption that people can work cooperatively to solve their problems constructively.

Getting on with

Dr. Franklin Ernst, a California psychiatrist, used the life positions to develop what he calls the "OK Corral" shown in Fig. 21.1.

The windows in the corral show my methods of resolving (or responding to) encounters with other people when I'm in each of the life positions.

If positive encounter involving negotiations, communications, and persuasive transactions with others is critical to my success in achieving career goals, it's obvious that only in the I'm OK-You're OK (get-on-with) position will I make much progress.

The I'm not OK-You're OK (get-away-from), I'm OK-You're not OK (get-rid-of), and I'm not OK-You're not OK (get-nowhere-with) positions are all major counterproductive barriers to progress.

Fig. 21.1   The OK corral (From Franklin H. Ernst, Jr. "The OK Corral: The Grid For Get On With," *Transactional Analysis Journal,* October 1971, p. 33. Copyright 1971 by the International Transactional Analysis Association, Inc. Reprinted by permission.)

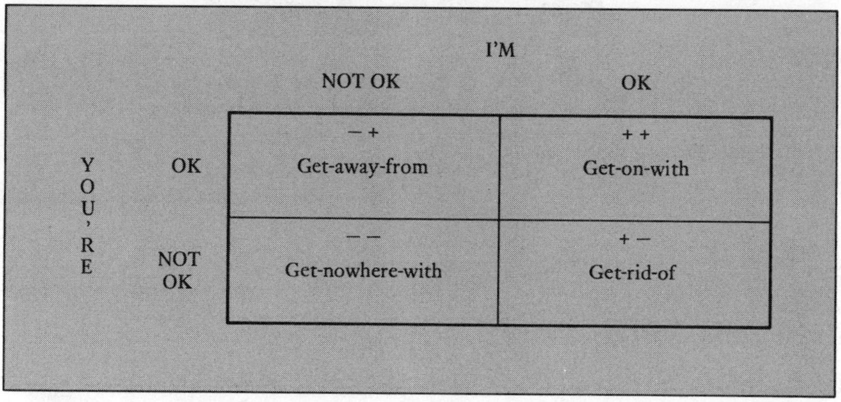

		I'M	
		NOT OK	OK
Y O U ' R E	OK	− + Get-away-from	+ + Get-on-with
	NOT OK	− − Get-nowhere-with	+ − Get-rid-of

The more time I spend in OKness, the higher the likelihood I'll succeed in getting what I want.

Most of us spend a great deal of nonproductive time in energy-wasting not-OKness. Why, and what can we do about it? The most exciting answer I've found to these questions comes from discoveries made by Dr. Taibi Kahler, another California therapist in the T.A. school of thought.

Drivers, discounts, and allowers 22

Counterproductive patterns

In working with clients, Kahler has identified five predominant compulsive-behavior patterns in our culture.[2] These patterns, which he labels Drivers, are based on unrealistic, counterproductive Parent messages. Each Driver has its own accompanying internal discount which leads to feelings of not-OKness, and inhibits my ability to find real satisfaction in life (if I choose to be dominated by the unrealistic demands of my Drivers).

Kahler's five Drivers and their accompanying Internal Discounts are:

Drivers	Internal Discounts
Be Perfect ⟶	No one can ever be perfect. It's impossible.
Try Hard ⟶	Don't do it. Just try.
Please Me ⟶ *(Please everyone)*	You can't ever please everyone. It's impossible.
Be Strong ⟶ *(Don't have or show feelings)*	Everyone has feelings. It's impossible not to have feelings.
Hurry Up ⟶	Don't take (or allow yourself) time to enjoy anything.[3]

We all have all the Drivers, but we rank order them differently, depending on our backgrounds.

Accompanying scripts

Berne found that each of us, whether we are aware of it or not, has a life script based on childhood decisions which we act out compulsively day to day much as an actor performs a play.[4] Kahler has found that how we rank order our Drivers determines what kind of a life script we are likely to have.[5] For example, if I rank "Be Perfect" as my number-one Driver, I'll probably have an "until" life script: "You can't be OK *until* you are perfect."

The specific life scripts associated with each number-one Driver are as follows:

Number-one driver	Probable life script
Be Perfect	*Until*—You can't be OK until you are perfect.
Try Hard	*Never*—You can try but you'll never be OK, make it, have fun, or really succeed at anything.
Please Me	*After*—You can be OK for a while but you'll pay the price. After you have fun the bad will come. Someone, somewhere, will not be pleased.
Please Me and *Try Hard* as number-one and number-two Drivers (in either order).	*Almost*—You'll almost make it and be OK but you won't quite succeed.
Hurry Up and *Be Strong*	*Always*—If that's what you want you can spend the rest of your life doing it.[6]

While "Hurry Up" and "Be Strong" are commonly observed Drivers in the *Always* script, there does not appear to be a consistent Driver ranking for this script.

Minute-by-minute defeaters

Each time we enter into a Driver we begin a very predictable sequence of events which Kahler calls our Miniscript.[7] (See Fig. 22.1.)

There are OK and not-OK Miniscripts which we repeat hundreds of times in our minute-by-minute transactions every day. This is what reinforces our life scripts and perpetuates them.

In the Miniscript sequence our Driver (e.g., "Be Strong") is followed by a Stopper (i.e., a personal internal script injunction such as

Fig. 22.1 The not-OK Miniscript (a roadmap for maintaining my impasses, and dissipating my energy for productive change) (From Taibi Kahler with Hedges Capers, "The Miniscript," *Transactional Analysis Journal*, January 1974, p. 31. Copyright 1974 by the International Transactional Analysis Association, Inc. Reprinted by permission.)

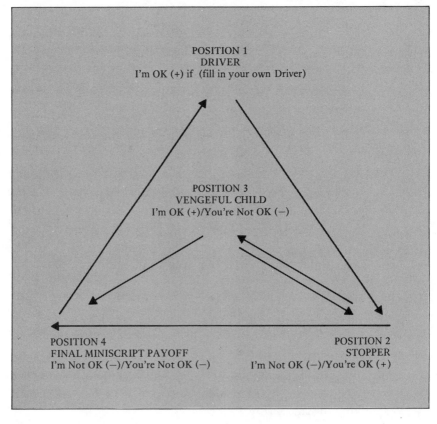

POSITION 1
DRIVER
I'm OK (+) if (fill in your own Driver)

POSITION 3
VENGEFUL CHILD
I'm OK (+)/You're Not OK (−)

POSITION 4
FINAL MINISCRIPT PAYOFF
I'm Not OK (−)/You're Not OK (−)

POSITION 2
STOPPER
I'm Not OK (−)/You're OK (+)

"Don't Feel") resulting in the accompanying internal discount (e.g., it's impossible to not have feelings). Our frequent reaction is then to "invite" others to share in our Drivers and in our not-OKness (e.g., If I can't "Be Perfect," I invite you to "Be Perfect." You can't do it either, so neither of us is OK.).

Losing sequences

The not-OK Miniscript shown in Fig. 22.1 moves ahead in a specific and predictable sequence as follows:

Position 1 *Driver*	I'm OK (+) if _____. Fill in the blank with the Driver (e.g., I'm OK *if* I can "Be Perfect" or "Please Everyone").
Position 2 *Stopper (leading* *to Internal* *Discount)*	I can't "Be Perfect," "Please Everyone," etc. It's impossible. Recognizing this I feel I'm not OK (−) and You're OK (+). That is uncomfortable, and I want to move out of this position. This leads to:
Position 3 *Vengeful Child*	I move into my Vengeful Child and invite you to "Be Perfect," "Please Me," etc. (Examples of how I might do this inviting are shown in Table 22.1.) You can't do it either. For a brief moment I can fool myself into believing I'm OK (+) and You're not OK (−), but this unreal position can't last so:
Position 4 *Final Miniscript* *Payoff*	I return to the feeling I'm not OK (−) but conclude you're still not OK (−) either. I can conclude it's hopeless (or move into whatever other favorite negative emotion I prefer) and quit trying. We "get-nowhere-with" each other.

At Position 3 (Vengeful Child), I invite you to share my unique prime Driver, whatever that is. If it's "Be Perfect," I invite you to "Be Perfect." A "Please Me" invites you to "Please Me." "Try Hard" invites you to "Try Hard"; "Hurry Up" invites you to "Hurry Up"; and "Be Strong" invites you to "Be Strong." (See Table 22.1.)

Note that when in my Miniscript I "invite" you. I can never "force" you to share my compulsive Driver. Being autonomous, you can choose to accept my invitation or to reject my invitation, keep

Table 22.1 Not-OK invitations
(We invite others to partake of our Drivers and Scripts*)

"Be Perfect" driver	"Try Hard" driver	"Please Me" driver (Please everyone)	"Be Strong" driver (Don't have or show feelings)	"Hurry Up" driver
Internal discount	*Internal discount*	*Internal discount*	*Internal discount*	*Internal discount*
If I'm not perfect I won't be OK (and it's impossible to be perfect).	If I don't try hard I won't be OK (if I can do it, it isn't hard enough to make me OK so I shouldn't do it; I should just try)	If I don't please everyone I won't be OK (and it's impossible to please everyone).	If I'm not strong, if I have and show feelings, I'll be vulnerable and I won't be OK (and it's impossible not to have feelings).	If I don't hurry, if I take time to really experience, I won't be OK (so I shouldn't take time).
Active expression	*Active expression*	*Active expression*	*Active expression*	*Active expression*
Use big words when little ones will do. Heavy on qualifiers. Covers all bases (of course, obviously, I think). Start sentence, interrupt and make insertion to clarify a point, finish sentence.	Doesn't finish sentences. Vocabulary full of words like "try," "difficult," "don't know," "Will work on it." Repeats questions. Doesn't answer directly. Asks second question before first is answered.	Talks in a whine. Turns statement into a question by raising tone at the end. Positive followed by a negative in sentence sequence. Start out talking about good feelings—insert "but" end with a negative.	No specific sentence pattern. Rigid, plastic face. Monotone.	Talks and moves quickly. Active body movements (tapping fingers or toes). Interrupts sentences of others to speed them up. Looks at watch.

* This table was developed from notes taken in a "Miniscript" workshop given by Taibi Kahler in San Diego, California, August 1974.

Table 22.1 *Continued*

"Be Perfect" driver	"Try Hard" driver	"Please Me" driver (Please everyone)	"Be Strong" driver (Don't have or show feelings)	"Hurry Up" driver
Not crisp. Gives more information than needed. Makes certain you understand perfectly. Detailed. Pedantic.	Hesitates in talking. You have to draw out and "Try Hard" to understand this person.	Raises eyebrows. Nods—Looks for "How am I doing?" Asks a question that isn't a question. ("That's red?")		Lots of suppressed feelings (e.g., anger, hostility).
Script invitation Invites you to "Be Perfect." "Precisely what do you mean by that?" "Whether or not 2 + 2 = 4 is a function of your base system. What is your base system? Exactly how did you figure that?" "Do you understand specifically what I'm saying?"	*Script invitation* Invites you to "Try Hard." Asks two questions without getting answer to first. (Try hard to respond.) Doesn't finish sentences. (You guess or finish for him or her.) Vague speech. (Try hard to understand.) Throw out a problem but don't request specific assistance. (I'm thirsty/ I'm hot.) "Do me something."	*Script invitation* Invites you to "Please Me." This is so (OK?) and that (OK?)—Tell me I'm right. Answers question with a question. "Could you"—"Would you" as opposed to a straight "Will you." Smile or nod for approval. (Please me by approving.)	*Script invitation* Invites you to "Be Strong." Remains rigid and unresponsive. (Keep feelings out of this.) Projects causes of feelings outside self "It makes me feel..." Stoic. (You be stoic too.)	*Script invitation* Invites you to "Hurry Up." Finishes your sentences for you. Looks frequently at watch. Fidgets nervously. Interrupts.

your transactions straight, stay out of my Miniscript, and instead invite me into your OKness.

When in my Miniscript I may choose to skip the Position 3 (Vengeful Child) step and simply move from Position 2 (Stopper) into Position 4 (payoff in not-OKness).

The not-OK Miniscript sequence can be completed in a minute or less. The payoff is always "get nowhere," and we repeat it hundreds of times a day. I was skeptical about this until I spent a week with Dr. Kahler in California and watched myself and other workshop participants leading each other habitually, again and again, through our Miniscripts on videotape.

Minute-by-minute helpers

I was glad to learn from Kahler and Dr. Hedges Capers, Kahler's cotrainer in the workshop I attended, that the not-OK Miniscript habit pattern is not irreversible. There is an OK Miniscript that I can use to keep myself in OKness and to "get on with" living my life the way I want to live it.

If I can learn to recognize and stop my Drivers, I can cut off escalation to Positions 2, 3, and 4 and stay in productive OKness.

Table 22.2 shows typical words, phrases, tones, gestures, postures, and facial expressions associated with the four Drivers. If I monitor my Driver behavior patterns and words, sentence by sentence, I can eliminate my Drivers and substitute corresponding "Allowers" for positive Miniscript behavior to reinforce OKness.

In addition to its accompanying Internal Discount, each Driver also has its own positive counteracting Allower as follows:

Driver	Positive counteracting allower
Be Perfect	*Be yourself.* It's OK to make mistakes. No one is perfect.
Try Hard	*Do it.* You don't have to just try. It's OK to go ahead and do what you want to do.

Driver	Positive counteracting allower
Please Me (*Please everyone*)	*Please yourself*. Respect yourself. Take care of your own needs. It's OK *not* to please everyone else. No one can please everybody.
Be Strong (*Don't have or show feeling*)	*Be open.* Accept your own and others' feelings. Feelings are OK. Everyone has feelings.
Hurry Up	*Take your time.* Live in the now. Enjoy. Relax and take enough time to do it right.[8]

Winning sequences

The OK Miniscript shown in Fig. 22.2 also has four positions and moves ahead in a predictable sequence.

Position 1 Allower	*I'm OK.* It's OK for me to be imperfect, make mistakes, do things, please myself, experience openness, and take my time to enjoy life.
Position 2 Goer	*You're OK.* It's OK for you to make mistakes, please yourself, do things, be open and take your time.
Position 3 Be'er	*I'm OK-You're OK.*
Position 4 Wower	*We're OK.* We can each be our OK selves and "get on with" our lives and each other.

If I stay in my OKness, that "invites" you to stay in your OK-ness in my presence. That is the most beneficial thing I can do for another person.

A manager who stays OK invites subordinates to stay OK and vice versa.

Table 22.2 The Miniscript chart*

Drivers:	Compliance (Inner feelings)		Psychological: internal discount†	Important behavior				
	Physical			Words	Tones	Gestures	Posture	Facial expressions
1. Be Perfect	tense		"You should do better."	"of course" "obviously" "effica-cious" "clearly" "I think"	clipped righteous	counting on fingers cocked wrist scratching head	erect rigid	stern
2. Try Hard	tight stomach tense shoulders		"You've got to try harder."	"It's hard" "I can't" "I'll try" "I don't know"	impatient	clenched, moving fists	sitting forward elbows on legs	slight frown perplexed look
3. Please Me	tight stomach		"You're not good enough."	"you know" "could you" "can you" "kinda"	high whine	hands outstretched	head nodding	raised eyebrows looks away
4. Hurry Up	antsy		"You'll never get it done."	"we've got to hustle" "let's go"	up and down	squirms taps fingers	move quickly	frowning eyes shifty

* From Taibi Kahler with Hedges Capers, "The Miniscript," *Transactional Analysis Journal*, January 1974, p. 37. Copyright 1974 by the International Transactional Analysis Association, Inc. Reprinted by permission.
† Suggested by John Kesterson

Table 22.2 *Continued*

	Compliance (Inner feelings)		Important behavior			
	numb rigid	"You can't let them know you're weak."	"no com- ment" "I don't care"	hard monotone	hands rigid arms folded	rigid one leg over	plastic hard cold
5. Be Strong						
Stoppers:						
Vengeful Child:						
Final Miniscript Payoff:						

Fig. 22.2 The OK Miniscript (From Taibi Kahler with Hedges Capers, "The Miniscript," *Transactional Analysis Journal*, January 1974, p. 34. Copyright 1974 by the International Transactional Analysis Association, Inc. Reprinted by permission.)

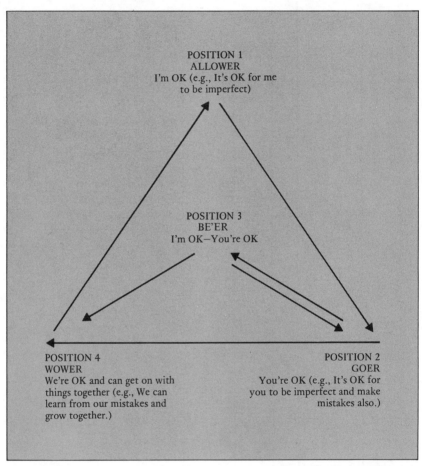

Carefully watching the Miniscript dynamic as it unfolds minute by minute when people communicate with each other in an organizational setting (meetings, interviews, appraisals, career discussions) can yield some really amazing insights on why some people "get on with" achieving their values and others "get nowhere," often in the same environment.

Carefully monitoring my own Miniscript behavior can be a tremendous boost in overcoming barriers, breaking through impasses, and "getting on with" my own career growth through quid pro quo negotiations and communications with relevant others.

Coping effectively

Understanding Miniscript theory and diagnosing my own and others' Drivers also makes me much more objective, tolerant of, and able to cope with other people's foibles. Whatever they are demanding of me ("Be Perfect," "Hurry Up," etc.), I can now realize they are making the same demands, probably much more sternly and forcibly, of themselves. Recognizing Drivers makes my Adapted Child far less vulnerable to other people's scary Controlling Parents. I can realize that most of the criticism people try to project onto others is really directed at themselves. My Adult can cope with this kind of criticism without getting upset or defensive. By staying in my own OK Miniscript I can refuse to be led into others' not-OK Miniscripts, invite others by example into OKness, and get on with our mutual positive goals when they accept the invitation.

Repertoires
for persuasion   23

Some practical tools

I mentioned earlier that lack of interpersonal competence (and confidence) is a major barrier to negotiating self-fulfilling work in an organizational environment. Few people are intuitive Process experts. Most have worked hard and consciously at developing their persuasive skills and interpersonal techniques.

Developing good interpersonal insights and a practical set of diagnostic tools for assessing what's really going on in the Process dimensions (within me, within others, and between us), and expanding my repertoire of persuasive interpersonal communications techniques is critical to negotiating value-fulfilling contracts.

That's easy to say, but how do I do it? Here again, T.A. gives us some very practical and specific tools to use. Miniscript awareness is one of many T.A. techniques I can use to increase my interpersonal communications skills. Let's look at some others.

Diagnosing the impasses

When communications between people are breaking down, are not taking place at all, or are locked in time-consuming, repetitive, nonproductive patterns, I can learn a great deal about what's going wrong and what I can do about it by analyzing the transactions taking place.

> The unit of social intercourse is called a transaction. If two or more people encounter each other . . . sooner or later one of them

will speak or give some other indication of acknowledging the presence of the other. This is called transactional stimulus. Another person will then say or do something which is in some way related to the stimulus and that is called the transactional response.[9]

Transactions take place between people, or as we said earlier, between the ego states of the individuals communicating. When I'm speaking with another person, there are ten ego states potentially involved: the Controlling Parent, Nurturing Parent, Adult, Adapted Child, and Natural Child for both myself and the other person. There are many opportunities for breakdown and, fortunately, just as many opportunities for recovery.

Berne taught us to diagram transactions between people using two columns of circles representing their ego states. If I ask Judd an Adult-to-Adult question ("Do you know where the McCabe report is?") and a tired, preoccupied Judd gives me a Controlling Parent-to-Adapted Child response ("It's your job to know that. You'd lose your head if it weren't attached.") communications would deteriorate, and I would diagram the breakdown as shown in Fig. 23.1.

Fig. 23.1   Crossed transaction

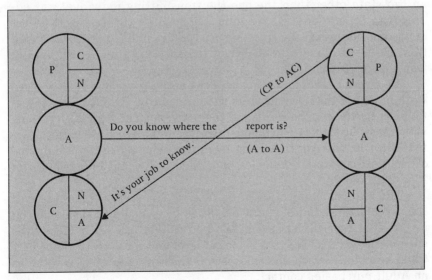

Three types of transactions

There are three types of transactions between people:

- complementary

- crossed

- ulterior[10]

Complementary transactions are those in which the vectors are parallel. This means that when I transmit a message to another person, that person responds from the ego state I intended to receive the message, and directs his or her reply to the ego state from which I am transmitting. If in the above example Judd had answered my Adult/Adult question with an Adult/Adult response ("I saw the report yesterday on John's desk.") our transactions would have been complementary. It doesn't make any difference which direction the vectors take in a complementary transaction so long as the vectors remain parallel (e.g., CP-to-AC transmission and AC-to-CP response). (See Fig. 23.2.)

A *crossed transaction* takes place when the vectors are crossed. Vectors are crossed when the responder unexpectedly answers from an ego state other than the one the transmitting individual was addressing. In our original diagram (Fig. 23.1) the transaction was crossed. I addressed my question to Judd's Adult and he responded from his Controlling Parent. When transactions are crossed, lines of transmission break down.

An *ulterior transaction* involves the activity of more than one ego state in one or both participants simultaneously. An ulterior transaction has *two levels,* the *social* and the *psychological.* An ulterior transaction may be *duplex* (involving more than one ego state in both participants) or *angular* (involving more than one ego state in only one of the participants). Examples of both types would be as shown in Figs. 23.3 and 23.4.

The real communication in an ulterior transaction takes place at the psychological, not at the social, level. The experienced salesperson in Fig. 23.4 (socially speaking Adult-to-Adult) has really kicked the customer's Child at the psychological level and received the hoped for Child response, which the salesperson then accepts at face value as an Adult purchasing contact.

- *As long as the vectors are parallel (complementary) communications can proceed indefinitely.*

- *If the vectors are crossed, communication is broken off. Conversely, if communication is broken off, there has usually been a crossed transaction.*

Fig. 23.2 Sample parallel vectors for complementary transactions

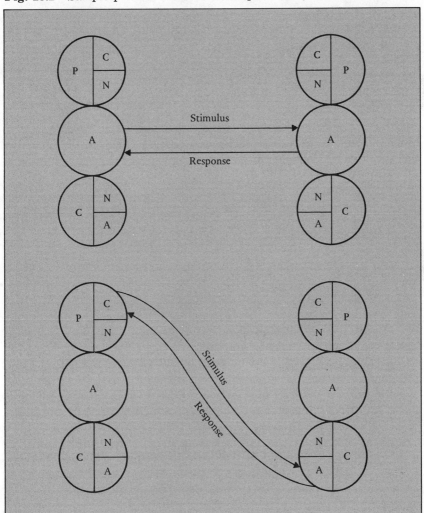

Fig. 23.3   Duplex ulterior transaction

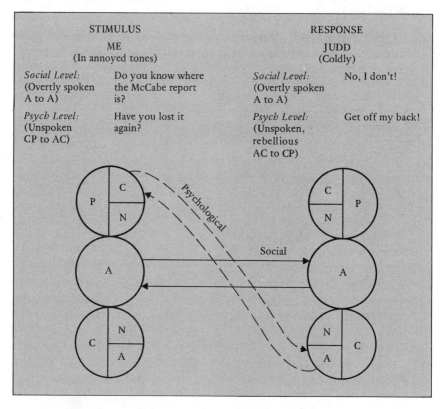

We don't conclude from this that complementary transactions are always to be desired (good) and crossed transactions are always to be avoided (bad). Whether I want to continue communications or break off communications becomes an Adult decision based on whether the specific communications in question are productive (getting me on in directions that I want to go), counterproductive (getting nowhere), or neutral (e.g., pastiming at parties).

If my wife is trying to communicate with me Adult-Adult (to solve problems rationally) or Child-Child (to have fun) and I'm continually crossing her transactions by criticizing her Adapted Child with my overly stern Critical Parent, it's time to work on uncross-

Fig. 23.4   Angular ulterior transaction

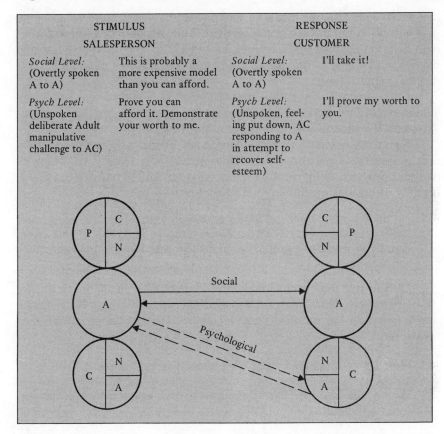

STIMULUS SALESPERSON		RESPONSE CUSTOMER	
Social Level: (Overtly spoken A to A)	This is probably a more expensive model than you can afford.	*Social Level:* (Overtly spoken A to A)	I'll take it!
Psych Level: (Unspoken deliberate Adult manipulative challenge to AC)	Prove you can afford it. Demonstrate your worth to me.	*Psych Level:* (Unspoken, feeling put down, AC responding to A in attempt to recover self-esteem)	I'll prove my worth to you.

ing our transactions and opening up some parallel communication channels.

If my manager keeps using his or her Controlling Parent to block me from promotions and training I want, and I keep on acquiescing from my Adapted Child, channels remain open and we have plenty of parallel communications but I'm at an impasse. It's time to cross the transaction as diplomatically as possible and get things moving in more productive directions.

Creative options

So what does this all mean to me? It means I have options. If one method of communicating, negotiating, and persuading someone who can help me achieve career values isn't working, I can analyze the situation and develop numerous other communications options to get things going my way.

I first learned about the exciting potential of conscious, deliberate communications options development in an article written by Dr. Stephen Karpman for the *Transactional Analysis Journal.*

Karpman noted that many people get locked into nonproductive communications patterns with other people and that T.A. "offers a simple approach to figure out what's going on, and illustrates the great variety of options available."[11] He also observed that:

> ... people who don't get along with many people in the world are limited in their range of possible responses. Anxiety, in this case, would be inversely proportional to the number of options a person has.[12]

During my oral exam for advanced membership in the International Transactional Analysis Association, the examining board gave me a question on options. They set up a hypothetical situation and asked me:

- How I would respond from each of my five ego states.

- Which ego state in the other person each response would be intended to hook.

The situation was as follows:

When you return from this exam your manager, a relative stranger recently assigned to supervise your work, calls you in and says:

> I let you finish your exams because I felt your former manager had made a commitment that you could. However, now that you are back, I'd like to make my views clear. I'm not an advocate of T.A. or any of the behavioral sciences approaches to manpower consulting. They waste time and are unproven. I want concrete results. I don't want you talking about T.A. or career planning in your future work with clients. Just stick to the bread and butter issues of recruiting, compensation, and union relations.

Some of the possible response options I gave were:

My Transmitting Ego State ⟶	Response	Ego State I Intended to Hook In the Manager
Option 1 *Critical Parent*	You should keep yourself more up-to-date on new developments. Obviously you don't understand T.A.	*Adapted Child*
Option 2 *Nurturing Parent*	You sound as though you've had some bad experiences with behavioral concepts. It's tough to get burned when you're trying new ideas isn't it?	*Adapted Child*
Option 3 *Adult*	Can you tell me a bit more about your concerns so I'm sure I understand them? What is it about the behavioral sciences you object to?	*Adult*
Option 4 *Adapted Child*	Yes sir. Thank you for letting me attend. I'll be careful not to inject these things into our consulting now that I know how you feel.	*Critical Parent*
Option 5 *Natural Child*	(Playfully) OUCH!!!	*Bull's Eye (hooks all 5 ego states)*

Actually, the above are rather simplistic, single-purpose responses. If I were a practiced option developer I'd move into advanced options involving multiple-part responses designed to hook more than one ego state in a carefully designed sequence of my choosing. I could say:

Multiple response	Ego states involved
You sound upset (crisply) (followed by)	*Controlling Parent* (bosses should stay calm) designed to switch him from the Controlling Parent to the Adapted Child ego state.
I sense you've been burned by subordinates using untested ideas in the past. I know how difficult that can be (followed by)	*Nurturing Parent* designed to soothe the boss's Adapted Child (I understand).
Can you tell me more about your concerns so I can understand and respond to them better?	*Adult* designed to hook the boss's Adult in an I'm OK-You're OK, data-based problem-solving mode.

I haven't agreed to the boss's restrictions. I've used options to keep the question open, hook his OK Adult, and collect data. What options I choose to use as the conversation continues would depend on what conclusions my Adult reached in processing the data as the conversation progressed.

Used properly (coming from my I'm OK-You're OK self with honest, productive communication as my motive) this is not devious manipulation, phony role playing, or "pretending." The roles are real, and they all truly represent me (my actual ego states). This is switching among different attitudes I already have toward the other person (my different ego states).

In advocating the positive use of options to break communications impasses and allow people to get on with positive, mutually beneficial progress, Karpman says:

> There is no talk of winning or losing, or acquiring sociopathic defenses, or learning to play a better game of *Now I've Got You, You S.O.B.* It just shows people the variety of their ego states and the ego states of others, how to reveal the different sides of

their personality and to appeal to the different sides of others, and to have a variety of tools to create a better communication.[13]

Practicing options (an exercise)

Table 23.1 and Fig. 23.5 show the instructions and the response form for an options-development exercise you can use to practice options development yourself. Follow this by outlining any real-life communications impasses that may be blocking you from getting on with your career. Develop options you can use to get things moving in the right direction. If possible, practice the options in a role play with your spouse or a friend before you try them on the actual person involved.

Table 23.1   Options exercise instructions

Situation:

You are aware of a promotional opportunity in another organization. You are interested and feel certain you qualify. You wonder why you haven't been asked to interview. You ask your boss about it. The response is as follows:

Boss: I'm aware of the opening. In fact, the hiring manager called and asked permission to interview you. I had to deny permission. Your skills are just too critical on our current program here.

Background:

Six months ago the same thing happened to you with the same boss.

Instructions:

Using the attached worksheet, write in five short possible responses you might make to the boss at this point. Each response should represent a different ego state in you responding (CP-NP-A-NC-AC).

Responses should be no more than three sentences each (and may be shorter).

Indicate which ego state in the boss each response is likely to hook.

Fig. 23.5   Options exercise worksheet

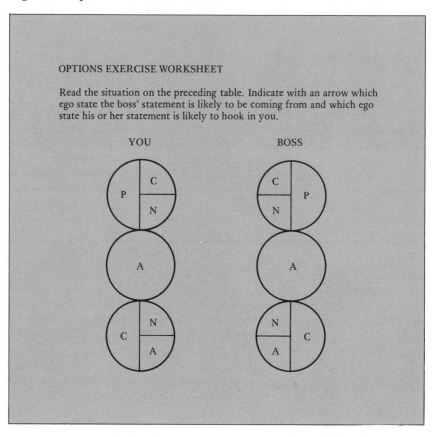

OPTIONS EXERCISE WORKSHEET

Read the situation on the preceding table. Indicate with an arrow which
ego state the boss' statement is likely to be coming from and which ego
state his or her statement is likely to hook in you.

YOU   BOSS

List below how each of your ego states might respond (i.e., what options
you have) and which ego state each response is intended to hook in the
boss.

Your response	Ego state likely to be hooked in boss
CP	
NP	

A	
NC	
AC	

Tell your role players not to give in and agree with you too early. Explain options and have them come back at you with every negative response option they can think of to block what you want. Develop new options to counter these negative responses. Try this with several different role players. Be a winner and learn from your mistakes. Then, thus prepared, take on the real-world situation. If you prevail, great. If you don't, learn from your mistakes and generate further options until you get what you want.

A bull's eye

Karpman tells us a "bull's eye" is an option that reaches all the ego states in another person.[14] A teenager who tells his or her parents, "I have to wait until you're in a better mood to tell you what happened with the car" might score a bull's eye. The parent's Controlling Parent is angry and the Nurturing Parent wants to calm the Child who is already upset. The Adult wants the facts; the Adapted Child is afraid to hear the facts; the Natural Child is curious and mischievously remembers having had a similar experience as a teenager.

You have a right

Karpman lists the following permissions we must understand and allow ourselves to take advantage of if we are to use options productively.

Permissions

- You have a right to demand straight transactions . . .
- You have a right to protect yourself . . .

- You have a right to express yourself . . . some . . . are frustrated because they can't say what they feel because their options are so limited.

- You have a right to learn options. . . .

- You have a right to use options . . .

- You have a right to see that others are using options. A person can see that all responses to him or her are not necessarily instinctive but may be decided upon . . .

- You have a right to see ego states correctly in others . . .

- You have a right to use all your ego states.[15]

Unrealistic and outdated Controlling Parent tapes in my head that forbid me to use the full repertoire of my ego states and options can cause severe roadblocks to achieving my career goals. Morally and positively using options to overcome counterproductive communications roadblocks is good for me and good for the people I communicate with. This is also very effective positive politics.

References

Part 6

Chapter 21

1. From Thomas A. Harris, *I'm OK-You're OK* (New York: Grove Press, 1967), pp. 37–53. Reprinted with permission.

Chapter 22

2. From Taibi Kahler with Hedges Capers, "The Miniscript," *Transactional Analysis Journal,* January 1974, p. 41. Copyright 1974 by the International Transactional Analysis Association, Inc. Reprinted by permission.
3. Lecture given by Taibi Kahler in a San Diego, California "Miniscript" workshop, August 1974.
4. From Eric Berne, *What Do You Say After You Say Hello?* (New York: Grove Press, 1972), p. 418. Used with permission.
5. From Taibi Kahler with Hedges Capers, "The Miniscript," *Transactional Analysis Journal,* January 1974, p. 41. Copyright 1974 by the International Transactional Analysis Association, Inc. Reprinted by permission.
6. Lecture given by Taibi Kahler in a San Diego, California "Miniscript" workshop, August 1974.
7. From Taibi Kahler with Hedges Capers, "The Miniscript," *Transactional Analysis Journal,* January 1974, p. 41. Copyright 1974 by the International Transactional Analysis Association, Inc. Reprinted by permission.
8. From notes taken in a "Miniscript" workshop given by Taibi Kahler in San Diego, California, August 1974.

Chapter 23

9. From Eric Berne, *Games People Play* (New York: Grove Press, 1964), p. 29. Reprinted with permission.
10. Ibid., pp. 29–34.
11. From Stephen B. Karpman, "Options," *Transactional Analysis Journal,* January 1971, p. 79. Copyright 1971 by the International Transactional Analysis Association, Inc. Reprinted by permission.
12. Ibid., p. 84.
13. Ibid., p. 83.
14. Ibid., p. 83.
15. Ibid., p. 85–86.

Perspectives

Part 7

It's fun *and* practical.

Personal fulfillment and self-reliance 24

No contradictions

We've stressed that success is a very personal thing which we all must define for ourselves. Success is not meeting the fluctuating expectations of others. Success is identifying my personal core values, and focusing my energy into channels that allow it to flow freely, naturally, and most effectively toward the realization of my values.

If I can do this, competence will come more easily because I really want it.

Too many people in our culture have untested erroneous Parent tapes that tell them pursuing personal values is impractical, and that people seeking personal fulfillment are selfishly chasing after rainbows leaving the real work and survival of the world to others. There are many who somehow see personal fulfillment as contradictory to pragmatic, reality-oriented self-reliance.

I believe there is no contradiction. I believe personal fulfillment can and should be the foundation and very essence of self-reliance. What is more self-reliant than identifying my strengths and using my available energies in the most efficient ways possible to build usable competence?

Competence precedes self-actualization

There are, admittedly, many self-deceiving souls in the world misusing the concept of personal fulfillment as a means of avoiding work and reality, hopelessly pursuing the impossible dream of a self-fulfillment or self-actualization that they incorrectly believe can be achieved without the hard work of developing competence. There can be, in fact, little self-actualization without competence and contribution, even for a Michelangelo who had to spend years developing the skills required to execute a *David* or a *Sistine Chapel.*

Hard work for high satisfactions

Personal fulfillment, no matter how you slice it, is hard work. Facing the tough reality that it is I (not some elusive Big Daddy or Santa Claus) who bear the responsibility for defining and achieving my goals, for navigating the direction of my own becoming, and for developing the competencies required to achieve my version of success is hard work. But, as we've said, this is not boring work. This is exciting, energy-generating work.

I have to spend (or structure) my time some way. Why not do it proactively instead of reactively?

For liberals and conservatives

Personal fulfillment and value achievement are not liberal standards to be used in battle against a conservative standard of self-reliance. Personal fulfillment and self-reliance when understood correctly are synonymous. As such, they should appeal to both liberals and conservatives. What better way is there to get things done and realize a very practical progress, than to have people learn to use their energies for maximum possible payoffs?

There can be no true personal autonomy without a solid foundation of competence and self-reliance.

The father of "self-actualization," the late Abraham Maslow of Brandeis University, made this point very clear in his "hierarchy of values" theory of motivation which has now become a classic in production-oriented industry.

Up and down
the pyramid 25

A hierarchy of needs

The late Douglas Murray McGregor of M.I.T. articulated the practical value of Maslow's discoveries for organizations and the world of work in his book *The Human Side of Enterprise.*

McGregor tells us that Maslow's pyramidal hierarchy of human needs (see Fig. 25.1) can explain a great deal about why and when we are and are not satisfied with the rewards we get from our work. The pyramid also explains why our satisfaction fluctuates from day to day.*

According to Maslow, we humans are wanting animals whose needs are never fully satisfied. Our needs, however, are not random. They are organized in a specific, ascending series of levels, a hierarchy of importance.

A satisfied need is not a motivator.† Food is not a motivator if I've just finished a big meal and am no longer hungry. Air, one of our most basic needs, normally motivates none of us as we walk about breathing freely and unconsciously. If I am suddenly deprived of air in a severe asthma attack or in a spaceship where the oxygen system fails, my need for air becomes very conscious and is the *prime motivator* of my life until the situation is resolved.

---

* From *The Human Side of Enterprise* by Douglas Murray McGregor, p. 36. Copyright © 1960. Used by permission of McGraw-Hill Book Company.
† Ibid., p. 36.

Fig. 25.1 Maslow's hierarchy of needs (From *The Human Side of Enterprise* by Douglas Murray McGregor, p. 36. Copyright © 1960. Used by permission of McGraw-Hill Book Company.)

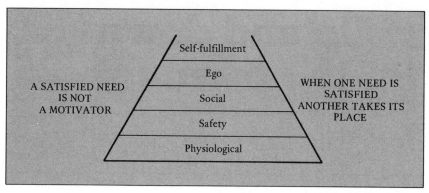

*When one set of needs is satisfied another takes its place** and I ascend, in specific predictable sequence, up to the next category of needs on the pyramid.

The five levels of needs (or motivational values) on Maslow's pyramid are, in sequence, *physiological, safety, social, ego,* and *self-fulfillment*.

Our most basic set of needs, the foundation of the whole pyramid, is *physiological*. "Man lives by bread alone when there is no bread."* Unless my basic requirements for food, air, water, rest, shelter, and protection from the elements are met at least at some minimum level, I think of nothing else. Unless I find some way to meet these needs, I won't be around long enough to worry about status, artistic achievement, or recognition.

Once my basic *physiological* needs are met, I move up the scale to my *safety* needs. Here, now that I've met today's pressing physiological needs, I begin to worry about the future. I take steps to assure I won't be deprived of the means to satisfy my physiological needs tomorrow, next week, or next year.

Some people refer to the safety needs as our *security* needs. It's a common mistake to believe our security needs can be met through a

---

* Ibid., p. 36.

passive dependence on others, whether "others" means an individual, an organization, the government, or society in general. No matter how benevolent they may be, if I depend on any "others" for my basic safety needs, I always run the risk that by chance, accident, or arbitrary whim, the "other" may withdraw support. That is scary, and it leaves me feeling insecure. The only real security is my own autonomy.

Safety, as described by McGregor, is the need for the "fairest possible break."* I want to believe that I, not some arbitrary other, control my own fate. I want to believe that what I do counts, that my actions are not irrelevant, that what I do and don't do really influences what happens to me.

Even at the basic levels a need for autonomy

Already at this very basic level there begins to emerge the need for autonomy, the need to free myself from the unknown whims of some ill-defined Big Daddy who can help or hurt me independently of what I do.

Once my safety needs are met at some minimum level I move up into my *social* needs. Here I become aware of my desires for belonging, for association with and acceptance by others. I want to give and receive friendship and love. A job that contributes to these as well as my *physiological* and *safety* needs is more rewarding than one that offers no social outlets.

Above my social needs I move into my *ego* needs. Here I start to become concerned with esteem at two levels.

First, I want *self-esteem*, the feeling of personal worth that comes from knowledge, competence, achievement, and a growing self-confident independence.

Second, *once I have self-esteem, I begin to want the esteem of others*. I want visibility, recognition, the kind of positive stroking that comes from being respected and admired by others.

A career that offers esteem in both dimensions will be more rewarding than one that doesn't. The esteem, of course, must come in my own value dimensions from competencies that have meaning for me. My Adapted Child striving to gain esteem by meeting other peo-

---

* Ibid., p. 37.

ple's expectations, especially if this thwarts or contradicts the achievement of my values, drops me right down to the fearful safety level of motivation.

At the top of the pyramid

At the top of the pyramid, when my *physiological, safety, social,* and *ego* needs have been met at some basic level, I move into the most rewarding level of all, *self-fulfillment.*

At the self-fulfillment level I become concerned with realizing my full potential, maximizing my personal growth and development, being creative in the fullest sense of the term. I strive toward fully appreciating and utilizing all my experiences for becoming the very most of what it's in me to be.

No one spends all his or her time in self-fulfillment, of course, not even the Einsteins and Michelangelos. Maslow says self-fulfillment represents our "peak experiences,"[1] those rare moments of ecstasy when we feel we have been for a brief period the very best of what we can be: when the violinist plays the perfect concerto and the scientist makes the most exciting breakthroughs.

Ecstasy isn't easy

So what does it all mean? For one thing, it means the ecstasy that comes from the peak experiences of self-fulfillment usually requires a lot of prior homework. I can't guarantee I'll ever get there, but I can significantly raise my probabilities of getting there if I develop a solid foundation of competence and autonomy.

It also means I'll have inevitable ups and downs. No one stays in the higher levels of the pyramid all the time. I can be all wrapped up in my social and ego concerns only to fall right back down to the safety level, hopefully temporarily, when natural or economic disasters hit. I've seen many an executive (temporarily) lose all concern for carpets, drapes, and preferred parking spaces when a major government contract cancellation threatened basic employment.

The pyramid tells me it's the nature of things for me to be striving for higher things and to be not completely satisfied when I get there. I prefer to leave the top of the pyramid open because no one ever achieves complete *self-fulfillment.* The structure of the pyramid gives me a framework for charting my ups and downs and for seeing both more calmly; realizing that even severe setbacks can be (and almost always are) temporary if I know the *name of the game* and keep on consciously and calculatingly plotting an upwards course.

Hopefully this book has given the reader a much clearer picture of the *name of the game.*

More than Utopia 26

All levels of the pyramid

The pyramid tells me that the techniques in this book are not all aimed at a utopian *self-fulfillment* perched only at the very top of the pyramid. These techniques are aimed at all levels of the pyramid.

Autonomy, identification of personal values, independence from the ill-defined Big Daddys of this world, and a calculated Adult plotting a course to release my Natural Child at its creative best are all very useful in meeting even my very basic *safety* and *social* needs. Certainly I want my criteria for meeting *ego* and esteem needs to be in my own, not someone else's value system.

Lastly, the more efficient release of energy, the relief from boredom and bottled-up tension, and the excitement and the sheer fun of finding it's possible to do things my way, and succeed, are all very good for my *physiological* well-being. I'm far less likely to become a tension statistic.

Who needs to be perfect?

It's even nice to know I can make many mistakes and still be OK. I don't have to Be Perfect, Please Everyone, Try Hard, Hurry Up, or even Be Strong. I can be imperfect, please myself, do things, have feelings, and take my time. I can fall flat, get up, and still grow. I will fall flat many times and there will be setbacks. Falling down can be my biggest growth experience of all so long as I always get up, learn, and maintain the forward momentum in directions I choose. This is what winners do.

References

Part 7

Chapter 25

1. From *Toward a Psychology of Being* by Abraham H. Maslow, © 1968, 1962 by Litton Educational Publishing, Inc., p. 67. Reprinted by permission of D. Van Nostrand Company.

Becoming your own Santa Claus

Part 8

It's exciting *and* effective.

Freedom, autonomy, and awareness 27

We've talked of *Response-Ability*, and that has really been the essence of this book. How do I develop my personal ability to respond effectively to life's challenges with freedom, autonomy, and a clear awareness of today's true realities?

How do I negotiate the maximum possible degrees of freedom to be what I want to be?

We have no magic formulas, but hopefully the insights and techniques we've presented will help you tune in to your own drummer, sort out the archaic tapes and no longer relevant voices and influences, and navigate your own zig-zag course for winning in your own very personally chosen dimensions of growth and success.

We've pointed out that anxiety about where you are and where you are going is very human. Anxiety needn't be avoided or suppressed as something bad. Anxiety can be your most important road signal for how to grow and find better things.

Anxiety can trigger a new awareness of realities. Awareness makes you periodically stop and notice where you are. Awareness lets you observe and experience your feelings and use them as clues to where you really want to go next.

Awareness gives your Adult important data to compute new, more exciting courses. With your Adult plotting a data-based course, it's less risky for your Natural Child to be spontaneous, to resist freezing the design, and instead to reach out for the new.

This is exciting. This is fun. This is effective. This is practical. This is becoming your own Santa Claus.

Appendix

It also pays off for the
organization.

Why industry needs more career-development programs

**Reasons improved career-development programs
can reduce rather than increase business costs**

Here are some of the reasons improved career-development programs
can reduce rather than increase business costs. Those readers who
work in personnel- and manpower-development functions might find
these arguments helpful in convincing line management there is a
need to try better approaches.

- People pursuing career goals that have personal meaning for them
  are more effective performers. They are more likely to stay with
  the organization (reduced replacement and orientation-training
  costs).

- Personal satisfaction and productivity are increased when people
  see their job activities as helping them achieve personal career
  goals (increased return on the payroll dollar).

- The demand for career autonomy, pursuit of personalized career
  paths, and organizational accommodation to different life-styles is
  increasing. The younger work force is demanding it. The need for
  meaningful individual/organization dialogue on these issues will
  continue to increase. (Organizations can't avoid this if they want
  to attract and retain strong people.)

Total attrition figures don't tell the full story

Total attrition figures for an organization don't tell the full story. A
low voluntary resignation rate among your professional population can

lead to a false sense of security. Look at the quality of the group that's leaving. Those people who make the self-effort and take the risk of looking for another job outside the company are frequently your top potentials—your entrepreneurs and self-starting creators. The mediocre and average performers seldom make the effort to change jobs unless they are forced. It's an old truism that if the environment doesn't foster growth and creative challenge, the good people leave. The average, the mediocre, remain forever.

Top-potential people who quit

I've done studies for organizations that showed this to be the case. Termination interviews with top-potential people who quit revealed a consistent pattern in their prime reason for leaving. This prime reason was: *lack of a perceived growth path.* They felt blocked or unrecognized. Sometimes they had been passed over for promotional opportunities because their contributions made them too valuable where they were.

How do you explain to people that they are so valuable they can't be developed or promoted? How do you sell people on a rationale that you appreciate their efforts so much, someone less valuable will have to get the promotion, extra salary, increased status, or developmental assignment? It's absurd. You can't. But managers try to do this regularly. They don't say it this bluntly. They smoke it up and appeal to loyalty with speeches that even convince themselves. Smart employees get the message, however, and the real self-starters eventually quit if this goes on very long.

How do you explain to people that although they are terrific the boss has peaked out so they'll have to bide their time waiting for an overdue promotion? How do you convince them that their personal needs can be pursued by staying on and back-stopping a boss's weaknesses instead of getting a job equal to the boss's somewhere else? If they are self-confident and independent you don't convince them. If you're smart you don't try to convince them. You open up new possibilities for them in your organization, or resign yourself to an expensive loss.

Lack of real selectivity in merit plans

Another reason top-quality people leave is lack of real selectivity in salary and merit-increase plans. At raise time the organization may be generous in the overall dollars it allocates, but supervisors and managers tend to avoid confronting the problem of separating the top performers from the average and the mediocre. Instead they give a little something to everyone. The hard-working top performer gets more, but not significantly more, than the average performer. The marginal performer, who may already be overpaid, gets at least something.

A quandary for the marginal employee

This puts the average and marginal performers in a quandary. Since they receive more than they deserve, why should they complain? Marginal performers are thus encouraged to avoid facing deficiencies in their performance because their supervisors find it difficult to discuss them. In the long run this can be very destructive to marginal employees. They become over-priced for what they do. This eventually becomes a problem to the organization and a threat to the individual's job security and marketability. It would have been easier to take corrective action if these individuals and the organization had confronted the performance deficiencies earlier, when the individuals concerned were younger. In a lower salary bracket, a move to something different would have been more feasible. These individuals might have become top performers in something they found more exciting, rather than marginal performers in something that bores them.

A quandary for the top performers

Top performers are quick to notice if their extra efforts are getting only minimal extra recognition and reward over average performers who coast along. Faced with this quandary they have two choices—

- *To continue their extra efforts despite the inadequate reward system.* This invites them to feel angry, bypassed, and put upon.

- *To reduce their performance to the average level—join the pack.* This invites them to feel depressed, guilty, underutilized, bored, and stifled. It invites them to quit growing.

Neither is a pleasant situation. If they really are top performers, their efforts to move on to another job in the same organization often meet a slow, polite, lip-service response from an immediate management reluctant to lose their talents.

Reduced productivity

Eventually the self-confident people in these situations look outside and quit. The average, marginal, less confident ones stay on forever, and their salaries slowly continue to rise. The organization expenses become too high for marketplace competition. Productivity goes down. This leads to personnel cutbacks (frequently the wrong, often creative, more junior people). The expense problem is relieved temporarily but the organization becomes less flexible and creative. It rigidifies. It slowly slips.

I've been able to demonstrate this pattern to client organizations and present dollar figures on the costs of hiring, moving, and training replacements for the high potentials who quit.

This got management's attention and approval for more systematic, open, and productive approaches to help people identify and meet their career goals within the organizational structure.

Personal career ownership can be an answer

This reduced attrition in critical categories because lack of a perceived growth path was a *much more critical* variable in causing good people to quit than salary dissatisfaction.

I haven't personally found a way to bring real selectivity to large organizational merit programs. Nevertheless, the overpriced, senior, marginal performer is more often than not a bored performer. If we could get more people to take personal ownership and responsibility for getting themselves into work that didn't bore them, we'd have far fewer marginal performers. Then the compensation problem would be less critical and productivity should increase significantly.

Index

Index